MANCHESTER STREETS

AND

MANCHESTER MEN

FIFTH SERIES.

By T. SWINDELLS.

WITH NINE ILLUSTRATIONS.

1908 :

PREFACE.

In publishing my fifth volume I must thank the large number of friends who by giving it their support as subscribers made its issue possible. The task of collecting the materials that go to make up a volume such as the present is a very great one, and it is very largely a labour of love. Having entered upon the work of telling the story of our city's growth, district by district, I should like to complete the record, but can only continue it so long as I receive the support of others interested in the work.

The many changes that each year sees made in our streets and their surroundings, coupled with the increasing difficulty of collecting data for volumes similar to the present one, make it desirable that the work should be completed without unnecessary delay. Future generations would seriously blame the present one, if it failed to hand down to them such particulars as are now available. This is proved by reason of the fact that to-day all persons interested in the story of our city's growth feel indebted to Whittaker, Aston, and Barritt for what they did.

It is now becoming generally recognised that the cultivation of an interest in local history is of national importance, and as the generations pass away this feeling will grow and develop. It is therefore with confidence that in issuing the present volume I ask for support for my next one, which will deal with Ancoats, Ardwick, and possibly Chorlton-on-Medlock. The work will be completed in seven volumes, the last of which will deal with Greenheys, Moss Side, and Hulme.

In the matter of illustrations I am again indebted to my friend, Mr. W. Ellis, and also to Mr. G. H. Rowbotham for valuable advice.

T. SWINDELLS.

MONTON GREEN,

ECCLES. *December*, 1908.

CONTENTS.

ILLUSTRATIONS.

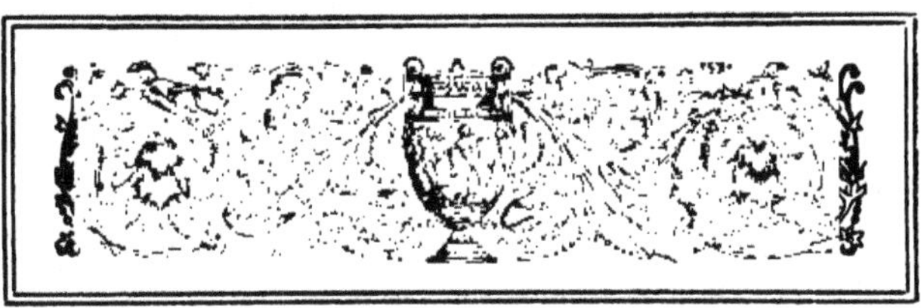

THE MAKING OF CORPORATION STREET.

Prior to the making of Corporation Street great inconvenience was caused by the absence of direct means of communication between Market Street and the rapidly developing residential district beyond Ducie Bridge. For foot passengers, acquainted with the narrow courts, streets and passages that lay between Market Street and Hyde's Cross on the one hand, and those from Hyde's Cross to Ducie Bridge on the other hand, there were several alternate routes; but for vehicular traffic there were only two roads to choose from: the one was through the Market Place, Old Millgate, Hanging Ditch, Fennel Street and Long Millgate, and the other was along New Brown Street, Shudehill and Withy Grove to Long Millgate. As the traffic of the town increased in volume the congestion in these thoroughfares, particularly on market days, became increasingly troublesome, and in the early forties the question of making a new street was seriously considered; and in August, 1845, the making of Corporation Street was commenced. At first it extended from Market Street to Withy Grove, and it was not until 1855 that the scheme was completed, and the Corporation Street as we know it was opened. It will be of interest to place on record the cost of the undertaking. The cost of the first portion after the proceeds for sale of remaining pieces of land, etc. had been deducted, was £47,530, and the second portion cost £40,588. The whole expense was exceedingly moderate as compared with the cost of a similar undertaking in the centre of the city to-day. Not only did the making of Corporation Street prove a benefit from the traffic point of view, but it helped to break up that mass of narrow streets and passages filled with old buildings, which in those days covered the area bounded by Market Street, High Street, Shudehill and Fennel Street, a fair sample of which remains to-day.

Sixty and seventy years ago most of the buildings in the area named were occupied as dwellings, although even then a change had commenced, and many of those situated near the principal streets had been converted into offices. Several of the streets and passages that suffered most by the making of the new street have already been dealt with in previous volumes, including Cockpit Hill half of which was removed, only the two ends remaining. Todd Street and Hanging Ditch have been referred to, as also have been Balloon Street, Miller Street and other thoroughfares running out of Long Millgate. One of those not already referred to, but which survived until 1885, should be mentioned. It stood on the right hand side of Corporation Street, a little way beyond Withy Grove, in fact, opposite the end of Todd Street and just before Balloon Street was reached. It bore the name of Clock Alley, a curious name for a curious collection of tumbledown buildings which, however pleasant and desirable as residences they may have been a few generations before, in our time were anything but pleasant and desirable. What they had been in the early part of the last century may be gathered from what Gregson said in 1833. In his *Gimcrackiana* he has a chapter headed Clock Alley, which I now reproduce.

CLOCK ALLEY.

"As this little place, or alley, took its name from rather a singular circumstance, not generally known to our readers, a brief account of it may not be uninteresting.

"Though it is only remarkable now for its general neglect, filthy appearance, and the depressing poverty of its inhabitants, it was, fifty or sixty years ago, as remarkable for a tenantry of an opposite description, though then consisting of the same classes as at present, of weavers, mechanics, etc., indeed, many of the present old tenants were born in the houses they now occupy; at which period the rents of their little tenements were only five pounds per annum, and subject to no imposts of any kind, either in taxes or other parochial assessments. But now, *tempora mutantur!* the same houses (though despoiled of their gardens) from the general change in the value of property, and the unfeeling cupidity of the landlord, have been advanced to £14 or £15 per annum, and are liable to all parochial rates and taxes.

"If the wages of the mechanics, etc. were then low, all the necessaries of life, as well as rents, bore the same low ratio in proportion, so that an industrious working man, if prudent in his conduct, could then live, enjoy most of the comforts, and even some of the elegancies of life. Nay, the very name of the place is a proof of this, as it had its origin from the circumstance that almost every inhabitant in the alley was then in possession of one of those useful, though now considered rather old fashioned, appendages in a house, an eight-days clock, which being at that time rather an expensive as well as elegant ornament, occupied a very conspicuous place in the lower or principal apartment of the house (which was not let off then, as it is now in various dwellings). Hence the name of Clock Alley; and even still, this article of furniture will be found in the houses of a few of the older and more respectable inhabitants, who yet retain their predilection for what they consider a sort of heirloom of the family, which passed probably to them from their father, if not their father's father, and such is the creditable feeling which still prevails among many of the older inhabitants of the place."

Such was the Clock Alley of 1833. What it was or what it appeared to Ben Brierley more than half a century later is equally worth recording. Writing on the eve of its demolition he said:

"This relic of a former Manchester is doomed. The fiat for its destruction is gone forth. The inhabitants have been "evicted" without the aid of the military or constabulary, and without the cry of "land-grabbing" being raised. It has had to make room for the extension of the wholesale department of the Co-operative Society. Situated in a part of Manchester that is growing in importance, it could have been foreseen long ago that 'Clock Alley,' like its neighbour, 'Cock Gates,' would as such disappear from the map.

"This locality has a history more immediately connected with the industries of Manchester than most people would give it credit for. Clock Alley especially has been noted in past generations for its fustian cutters and smallware weavers, and it is in connection with the latter that its name is supposed to have originated. There have been various ways of accounting for it. One statement—very improbable—is that every house at a time remote possessed an eight-day clock. Another story relates to an old woman carrying a clock case on her back to the nearest pawnshop. But the more likely way of accounting for the name is the fact that the smallware weavers were mostly engaged in producing 'clock-lace,' at one time very much used for military and other facings. Be that as it may, it will soon be a thing of the past.

"It would be something as a lesson to our 'jerry' builders to make an inspection of the walls of Clock Alley before they entirely disappear. They will find no single brick walls. All the interiors are double, and the setting does not appear to have been hastily done. The hod-carrier must have had plenty of time to do his share of the work. There is no sign of dilapidation except in the outer woodwork, which has not been extravagantly favoured with paint. There is nothing else that would lead anyone to suppose they were looking at the skeleton of an old human 'rookery.' All the signs of life—contented life—have now disappeared; the denizens of the rookery have been scattered. This has not been done without much mental suffering. To some of the inhabitants—old people, too—Clock Alley has been their only home; and that must account for the home feeling manifested on their departure from it. An old fustian cutter, who has spent half a century in his garret, fairly broke down on his being compelled to leave. All the associations of life were being separated from him. It is difficult for some people nowadays to enter into this home sentiment. They are here to-day and gone to-morrow, consequently home feelings never take root anywhere. But with such as have been reared in Clock Alley it is different. They would not have given up their urban homes for the bright attractions of a suburban cottage. In fact, as an old inhabitant told me, he only saw the country on a Sunday, and that was the time to enjoy it. The fields were greener to him than they were to those who lived amongst them; and he could enjoy a ramble in the old lanes much better than if they had been familiar to him. And on the score of health, what place could be healthier than where people lived until they had forgotten how old they were?"

The home feeling referred to by Mr. Brierley is still to be found in the neighbourhood of Corporation Street, although, consequent upon the changes of recent years, the number of old residents must be very small. In a letter received from a subscriber occurs the following sentences which are to the point. He says: "As your next book deals with Withy Grove and neighbourhood, perhaps you may mention Marsden's Court, off Fennel Street. There are two or three houses still inhabited there, one man having lived in the same house nearly fifty years. This is the last house round the bend at the top of the Court. I also know an old printer, nearly eighty-five years old, who was born and lived for over twenty-one years in this particular court."

THE SPREAD EAGLE HOTEL.

Another change produced by the making of Corporation Street was in connection with one of our old inns, the Spread Eagle. Formerly it was approached from Hanging Ditch, but the making of the new street gave an opportunity for securing a better frontage, of which the proprietor was not loth to avail himself.

The Spread Eagle Inn was said to have dated back to 1745, and it is stated that in connection with the "affair" of that year, the Duke of Perth and many other officers connected with the Pretender's army, stayed there during their visit to the town; and it is said that when the inn was rebuilt about 1836 a signet ring and other old valuables were found. If so, it would be interesting to know if any of those relics still survive, and if so, where they are.

In the coaching days an occasional coach would start from the Spread Eagle, but it was never recognised as a coaching house. The neighbouring inns, the Roebuck and the Old Boar's Head were more popular in that respect. The inn, however, had a fairly large connection with country manufacturers, who, coming to town on Market days, were in the habit of putting up at certain houses. Thus in the old directories will be found a long list of "Country Manufacturers, Spinners, Bleachers, etc. attending the Manchester Markets, the situation of their warehouses, days of attendance in Manchester, and the inns they put up at." Of this class of custom the Spread Eagle had a fair share. One of the early references to the inn has reference to it as a coaching house, in 1791, at which time a coach ran daily from there to Liverpool. On May 11th, 1791 the Court Leet ordered that William Whitehead, the proprietor of the Spread Eagle, be amerced in the sum of one pound one shilling, unless he removed the carriages and post chaises that he was in the habit of leaving in Hunter's Lane, to the annoyance and danger of His Majesty's subjects.

The inn was the scene of much excitement in 1819 prior to Peterloo. Hunt was in Manchester in the early part of that year, and stayed at the Spread Eagle. Whilst here he decided to visit the theatre in company with some of his friends. He was received with much cheering by a portion of the audience, to the annoyance of the Earl of Uxbridge and a number of the supporters of the government. In the end Hunt was forcibly ejected from the theatre, and accompanied by a large crowd returned to the Spread Eagle. Smarting under the indignity thus inflicted, he was again assaulted by a number of persons who forced themselves into his room. After this Hunt declared his intention of again visiting the theatre, and invited his supporters to form a sort of bodyguard. The authorities saw that serious disturbances would result from such a demonstration, and gave instructions that no performance was to be given on the evening, and notification of this was conveyed to Hunt at the Spread Eagle by Ryley the Itinerant, who was one of the performers at the theatre.

After the advent of the railway system the Spread Eagle, like many other inns, changed character somewhat, but unlike many of its contemporaries it continued to enjoy a fair share of popularity amongst commercial travellers and other persons periodically visiting the city. Its removal recently was the result of further street improvements, and as we stand to-day near its site, and look around we realise the tremendous changes that have taken place since the time when the Liverpool coach started from the inn in Hanging Ditch, and when narrow streets, dark courts, and crowded buildings covered the area now represented by wide thoroughfares.

Another well-known institution in Corporation Street for a number of years was the Trevelyan Hotel, which was conducted on temperance lines.

A TEMPERANCE PERIODICAL.

One of the best written temperance periodicals ever connected with the city was the *Manchester Temperance Reporter*, which had only a short but troublous career. The first number was published by A. Weston on August 1st, 1849, but after the issue of the fourth number it collapsed. It was, however, recommenced by Grant & Co., of Corporation Street, and was issued weekly for nearly six months, when it again suffered another change. Under a new regime it appeared as *The Temperance Reporter and Journal of Useful Literature*—a title high sounding enough to almost demand success. But the fact was that the temperance movement was only in its infancy, and a periodical with such a title, appealing only to temperance men, was almost certain to fail. After a few issues it ceased. A word or two may be said with reference to the contributors to the little journal. It was edited by S. Pope, the well-known Q. C., and J. Johnson, the former also contributing a series of articles on "Secrets of Success." The leading contributor was Alexander Somerville, of Whistler at the Plough fame. His contributions consisted of short stories and essays. One of the former: "The Merry Christmas which Came at Last," was reprinted in many newspapers, and was, in the opinion of Archibald Prentice, equal in pathos and descriptive writing to many of the best passages in Charles Dickens' works. Other contributors included A. Prentice, Dr. McKerrow, Dr. F. R. Lees, Dr. J. Wilkinson, J. Critchley Prince, and Elijah Ridings. With such a range of talent it is curious that the venture was a failure.

THE RELIGIOUS INSTITUTE.

The Religious Institute now located in Deansgate originated largely through the influence of John Fernley, a Stockport cotton spinner, who retired to Southport, and who in his will endowed the Fernley Lecture in connection with the Wesleyan Methodist Conference. The site cost £3,100, which was met by public subscription, but the building, which cost £4,000, was erected at the expense of Mr. Fernley. It was intended for the use of the Bible Society, the Religious Tract Society and the City Mission. In 1899 the property was sold, and the premises were rebuilt under sealed order of the Charity Commissioners at 135 Deansgate, where the work of the respective organisations is now carried on.

CHEETHAM HILL ROAD AND CHEETHAM HILL.

PART I.

In a work like the present one, although there are many temptations to extend the area of our investigations, it is essential that with a few special exceptions we should confine that area by certain limitations. In the present case we shall confine our references to that portion of Cheetham to the district bounded by the Manchester Municipal boundary as defined in the Charter of Incorporation of 1838, making an exception in the case of Heaton Park, an account of which will form the last chapter in the Cheetham Hill section of the volume.

The name of Cheetham appears to have been originally spelt with one e; and as such we find it referred to in a document dating back to the earlier part of the fourteenth century. In that document we read that: "Roger de Midleton holds one carve of land in Chetham, in chief of the lord the king in thanage by one mark," and that "Henry de Chetham holds all that land of the said Roger." By this we find that Roger de Midleton held the land probably comprising the area latterly known as the township of Cheetham, as tenant under the king, whose successor to-day is Duke of Lancaster; and that he sub-let it to one Henry, who evidently took his name from the estate or holding. Harland derived the name Chetham or Cheetham from two Anglo Saxon words, the first of which, Cedde or Ceot, was a Saxon male name, and the second ham meant a home or habitation. Whether this suggested derivation is the correct one or not the name Chetham or Cheetham, in common with hundreds of other English names was at the same time a place name and a family name. The Chetham family formerly held lands at Nuthurst, Butterworth, Middleton, Castleton, Crompton and elsewhere, the Humphrey Chetham branch being " descended from a younger brother of the blood and linage." Humphrey Chetham, the founder, was born at Crumpsall in 1580, and a century later a nephew of his died at Smedley.

A word may be said about the old hall, the birthplace of Humphrey Chetham, a view of which is here given. It was a fine, picturesque, black and white building, oblong in shape, with cross gables at either end. It was two storeys in height, and its high pitched roof was relieved at intervals by dormer windows. It was a quaint looking structure, its old fashioned bay-windows fitted with scores of diamond shaped panes of glass, being in striking contrast to the windows to be seen on the site to-day. Two views of the building are included in James's series, and judging from those pictures Crumpsall Hall a century ago must have been not only very pleasantly situated but a comfortable place to live in. The story of the hall may be briefly told.

Humphrey Chetham died unmarried, and the estates left by him passed to various members of the family.

Edward Chetham, who died in 1769, was the last male heir, and at his death his estates were divided between his two sisters. Crumpsall Hall was soon afterwards sold, and after changing hands several times, was purchased by Thomas Blackwall, who resided for some time at the present Crumpsall Hall. In 1825 the building was pulled down and villa residences with the name of Spring Bank were erected on the site. In more recent times the villas in turn have disappeared, and in their stead we have numbers of smaller habitations. The old building stood in Sandy Lane, now known as Crescent Road, near to the junction of that thoroughfare with Humphrey Street. When it was pulled down a secret staircase was discovered in the kitchen gable leading to a small chamber in the roof, supposed to have been used as a hiding place in unsettled times, and during periods of religious persecution.

An anonymous writer, describing the appearance of Cheetham Hill at the time the Hall was pulled down, gives some very interesting details of

CHEETHAM HILL EIGHTY YEARS AGO.

In the early decades of the last century Cheetham Hill was a quiet rural village, divided from Manchester by a roadway along which passed very little traffic. An occasional farmer's cart, or, perchance, a post chaise and the York mail, together with a few other coaches were the only vehicles that passed through the sleepy little village. At night the road was entirely unlighted and the number of houses between New Bridge Street to Halliwell Lane did not exceed a score, in all. There was little pedestrian traffic .after dark.

For those who were able and willing to pay the cost, a pair horse coach could be hired in St. Ann's Square. The fare, however, was five shillings to Cheetham Hill, but in addition to this toll bars cost eightpence, and the driver expected sixpence for a drink. Needless to say the pair horse vehicles from the town were not often seen in the village of Cheetham Hill. We are not surprised to read, therefore, that highway robberies were somewhat common in the twenties, but it was not until a Mr. Ruddock was shot that the better class inhabitants made a move towards making travelling along the highway more safe. A private watch was established, the watch consisting of two watch men of ancient type. Each of these carried a lantern and a heavy stick, and small watch boxes were placed, one at the Stocks, and one at Halliwell Lane. Persons out late at night would, if alone, wait at the corner of the workhouse for the watchman coming on his down beat, and he would accompany them along the road. In this connection a story of those days may be told. The apparitor of St. Mark's Church, who was usually clad in a brown coat with scarlet facings when on duty, being a man of venerable appearance, usually acted as escort for elderly spinsters on their way home from evening parties. "At the close of one of these parties—and they were neither tea-fights nor muffin struggles, but a good hospitable tea and supper together with a rubber of whist or a set of quadrilles—the servant announced 'th' 'Paritor's come for Miss W.' Miss W. said to Miss E. 'You are going my way,' which meant 'You can join at the escort.' The ladies put on their thick boots and pinned up their skirts. Each put her cap into a band-box, and replaced that precious article of female headgear with a 'calash,' a thing like the top of a hansom cab in miniature; and having girded themselves with an umbrella of dimensions and strength that would astonish the ladies of to-day, announced that they were ready. First, about three yards in front, walked the said official with a large lantern, and a stout stick; if the night was cold he had on his coat of many colours. Then came the elderly spinsters, tucked and pinned up as aforesaid. At intervals down went the lantern: 'There's a puddle, ladies!' exclaimed the attentive official. Then up went the lantern: 'Mind the stump!' Then down again: 'Be careful, ladies; here's a slide! Them boys wants punishing for making slides, they does.' And thus, with courteous attentions, the ladies were deposited at their respective homes." Such was the usual course of events, but on one particular night a confiding lady had entrusted herself to the care and keeping of the apparitor. All went well until a part of Halliwell Lane was reached where overhanging trees on either side of the road made the spot a favourable one for the perpetration of highway robbery and murder. Whether on the night in question the darkness was deeper than usual or not, or whether the guide was suffering from an attack of nervous depression deponent sayeth not, but just as they were passing under the trees he said to the lady: "Miss ———, it's very dark, aren't you fear'd?" "No, Harry," replied the dauntless spinster. "Well, I am!" said Harry, and off he set with his lantern as fast as his legs could carry him, leaving the lady to find her way home as best she could.

In those days Cheetham Hill had no doctor, and its limited range of shops included one bread shop but no butchers' shop. The residents relied for their supplies of flesh meat upon "Old Billy Kay," an itinerant butcher whose shop was in Miller's Lane. The cottages were few in number. Some were black and white and others were whitewashed, whilst in several cases thatched roofs added to the picturesqueness of their appearance. To most of them gardens were attached.

The licensed houses eighty years ago were the Griffin and the Bird in Hand. To the Griffin was attached a bowling green; and in the winter months balls were given in its largest room. In front of the Bird in Hand were water troughs for horses and near by were the stocks. The inn itself was one of the most picturesque in the neighbourhood, and when in recent times it was removed, one of the most interesting of local landmarks disappeared. Eighty years ago the Bird in Hand was the last house in the village, no other buildings being seen until Sandy Lane, now Crescent Road, was reached, where several substantial residences stood. At the corner of Middleton Road stood a toll bar which was known as the White Smithy bar because of the whitewashed smithy that stood on the opposite corner of the road.

SIXTY YEARS AGO.

Before another twenty years had passed away very great changes had taken place in Cheetham Hill and the road leading to it. From the corner of New Bridge Street to Stocks it was known as York Street, the name Cheetham Hill Road being limited to the length of roadway from there to the village.

In describing the thoroughfare as it appeared sixty years ago it should be noted first that the toll bar that had stood at Ducie Bridge was removed in 1830. Passing along the road it should also be noted that thus early the town was extending in the direction of Cheetham, for from the workhouse to Exchange Street on the left hand side several rows of houses had been built, although on the opposite side only a small amount of building had been done. A few houses at the corner of Derby Street, and York Place on the opposite side formed the only breaks in the fields that extended to Stocks House. Behind the houses at the bottom end of York Street a brick croft occupied a portion of what had been Strangeways Park, and close by was a bleachworks, the water supply for which was obtained from a one-time popular fish pond. Stocks house pleasantly situated, had not then lost its attractiveness, and on the opposite side of our thoroughfare was a farmer's lane known by the expressive name of Dirty Lane, now represented by Elizabeth Street. A little way up Dirty Lane was Snow Hill, just on the boundary line of Manchester and Salford. At Snow Hill were some fruit gardens, known popularly as Braddock's, where visitors could purchase fruit and assist in gathering it. The fruit garden and Dirty Lane disappeared about half a century ago and to-day we have a number of semi-detached and other houses ranged along Elizabeth Street, the echoes of which are roused all day long by the passage of the electric cars.

Leaving Stocks and Dirty Lane, Wilton Terrace would be passed. Built in 1836 the houses for many years overlooked open fields which extended right away to the village of Collyhurst. Behind the terrace more open fields with the pleasant village of Cheetwood on the one hand, and the wooded heights of Higher Broughton on the other, made residence there more than tolerable. Beyond Wilton Terrace there were very few houses, the land on either side of the road being devoted to agricultural purposes. The Temple and the Bowling Green connected therewith, together with St. Luke's Church formed an interesting group; the church, from its elevated situation, being a noticeable landmark. From St. Luke's to the end of the village a generation had made comparatively few changes, although the number of villa residences had grown somewhat. The village still preserved its old-time charm, and when the annual wakes came round its principal street was still paraded by groups of morris dancers accompanying the Rush cart in its progress

CHEETHAM HILL ROAD AND CHEETHAM HILL.

PART II.

SOME EARLY RESIDENTS.

JAMES RAWSON—THE ARCHER.

More than a century ago the village of Cheetham Hill was noted for the skill of certain of its natives in archery. The pastime was very popular with the residents, and long years after it had disappeared from all other parts of the Manchester district it was cultivated there. Pilkington's bow and arrow shop and Hyde's smithy at Sandy Lane, where an arrow could be tipped for a penny, were popular institutions, whilst the sign of the Robin Hood served to remind wayfarers and villagers alike of the prowess of Nottingham's famous outlaw.

The greatest of local bowmen was James Rawson, concerning whom few particulars have survived. Perhaps the best account of him was the one written by R. Wood in the *Manchester Guardian* in 1874. He says: "I fear I have little information to give concerning James Rawson, except what I have gathered from old people. Although some of them remembered him well, they were not very particular about telling the same story of his wonderful feats twice over without some variation. James Rawson was a handloom weaver and lived most of his life in an old house, now in ruins, opposite the Griffin Inn. Weavers were then well off and could afford to indulge in many amusements from which they have been debarred since the invention of patent looms and the introduction of steam power. Archery was then a favourite amusement, not only with the rich but with tradesmen and working people also. James appears to have begun shooting early, and even in boyhood to have acquired extraordinary proficiency, so that, as his grave stone has it, 'from 16 to 60 he never refused a challenge nor ever lost a match.' When he became too old to weave, the gentlemen employed him to attend on shooting days and keep their bows in order, and when they had a friendly match with other villages they would dress him up as a gentleman to take part with them so as to get the benefit of his score; and it is said that in one of these matches held at Prestwich, the affair was so well contested that James and his opponent, the two last players, were on equal terms, and the two last arrows had to decide the match. When the Prestwich man sent his arrow the game appeared settled, as it had struck within an inch of the centre of the target, and the shaft lay a little obliquely, so as to cross the centre. But James sent his arrow with such truth and force that it split the other one and struck the very place required. This was considered the greatest feat in archery since the time of Robin Hood. When he died the gentlemen archers attended his funeral, and paid all expenses, including that of a gravestone. Rawson was buried in St. Mark's Churchyard, where his gravestone with the following epitaph may be seen:

"Here were interred the earthly remains of
JAMES RAWSON,
who died October 1st, 1795; aged 80 years.
His dexterity as an archer was unrivalled; from the age of 16 to 60 he never refused a challenge, nor lost a match.

Grim death, grown jealous of his art,
His matchless fame to stop,
Relentless aimed th' unerring dart
And split the vital prop.
This favourite son Apollo eyed,
His virtues to requite,
Conveyed his spirit to reside
In realms of endless light."

THOMAS HENSHAW.

Thomas Henshaw, the founder, died on March 4th, 1810, at Stone Wall, a delightful old house that formerly stood opposite to the end of Halliwell Lane. Henshaw, who was of humble origin, was born at Prestbury in 1747. He settled in Oldham in 1775 and became very successful as a felt hat manufacturer. By his will he devised £20,000 each for the founding of a Blue Coat School at Oldham, and a Blind Asylum in Manchester. In a later codicil he increased the amount for the former institution to £40,000. The money was left for the maintenance of the institutions named, the testator anticipating that the funds requisite for the purchase of sites and the erection of buildings would be contributed by others. A lawsuit ensued, but in the end the legacies were declared to be valid. In 1834 a public subscription was opened to provide the funds necessary for the erection of a blind asylum to which was added a deaf and dumb school. The foundation stone was laid on March 23rd, 1836, by William Grant, and the building was opened on June 21st, 1837, with a public procession. Mrs. Henshaw widow of Thomas Henshaw, died at Stone Wall on April 8th, 1836. Their daughter married Edward Loyd, the banker, who resided at Greenhill, a mansion that formerly stood on Alms Hill. The house had been erected by Samuel Jones, the founder of the well-known banking concern, and whose sister married the Rev. Lewis Loyd, the Unitarian minister, who also became a partner in the banking business. Samuel Jones died at Greenhill in 1819 and the house was occupied by Edward Loyd for some years afterwards. An account of the family was given in my first volume.

JAMES CHETHAM—THE ANGLER.

A resident of the closing portion of the seventeenth century should be mentioned. James Chetham was a member of the Chetham family to which reference has already been made. He was born in Manchester in 1640, and died at Smedley in 1692. He is celebrated as the author of *The Anglers' Vade Mecum*, published in 1681. In his volume, which was published anonymously, he details some of his experiences in the "gentle art." In one place he refers to having eaten eels out of thirty several rivers "yet none that I ever met with were to be compared for goodness (although not large) and deliciousness of taste to the eels caught in a small river in Lancashire called Irk." He waxes eloquent concerning the merit of the inhabitants of the Irk, and says that the reason assigned for the superior excellence of the fish was the presence of the

Fulling Mills on the bank of the river whereby "the fat, oil, and grease scoured out of the cloth make the eels palatable, and far above other river eels." The first edition of the *Vade Mecum* was published in Manchester, but the second was published in London in 1689. The preface to this edition was signed "Jas. Chetham," and was dated from "Smedley, near Manchester, in Lancashire, November, 26th 1688." He gave his reason for disclosing his identity in quaint terms. He said that he "now annexes his name, not out of the Common Itch or Ostentation to be seen in Print, but to evidence that he is not ashamed to own the work, which although an Anonymous at First, yet from which Anglers found a generous entertainment." The book is now of value as a rarity, but it never enjoyed the popularity secured by Walton's more famous book.

CHEETHAM HILL ROAD AND CHEETHAM HILL.

PART III.

STOCKS HOUSE AND SOME OF ITS OCCUPANTS.

Stocks, or Stocks House as it was called in different periods of its history, stood opposite the end of Dirty Lane, now Elizabeth Street. Before the length of Cheetham Hill Road extending from New Bridge Street to Stocks was made the road to Cheetham Hill from the town was along Long Millgate, over Scotland Bridge and up Red Bank. As to the origin of the name "Stocks," or the extent of the estate connected with the house little is known. In Green's Plan of Manchester and Salford, published in 1794, Stocks is depicted as being a short distance past "Mile House." The estate appears to have extended about 130 yards east of the high road, and to have been about the same length from north to south. The outbuildings were numerous and the grounds were laid out in an ornamental manner with gardens, shrubberies, ponds and walks. One lake was serpentine in shape, and was about one hundred yards long, and appears to have been connected with the ornamental waters in Strangeways Park. In the centre of the plan of the Stocks estate is the name of "J. Rydings, Esq." the surrounding fields being marked as the Earl of Derby's.

The explanation of the latter statement lies in the fact that after the Battle of Bosworth Field the Manor of Chetham was taken from the Pilkington family, and granted to the Earls of Derby as a reward for valour.

At the time referred to (1794) Stocks was a fine, roomy mansion, one portion of which was three storeys high and another two storeys. It stood some little distance from the road, and just past it were the stables with the turret, which last named still survive, although devoted to a very different purpose from that for which they were intended. The first occupiers of Stocks of which we have any mention were members of the Rydings family. For more than two centuries they occupied the mansion or at any rate the estate, for the house as it appeared half a century ago was probably not more than a century old. In the Collegiate Church registers from 1573 to 1806 are many entries notifying the birth, marriages and deaths of various members of succeeding generations of the family. Thus we find that John Rydings, after burying an infant daughter in 1599 and his wife in 1601, was himself buried on May 4th, 1604. For two centuries the family seem to have lived in quietness; the name rarely appearing in connection with public work. It is not apparent whether the earlier members engaged in trade, but those belonging to later generations followed the occupation of merchants.

A shade of romance hangs over an announcement made in the *Manchester Mercury* for 1772 to the following effect: "September 2nd. On Wednesday last was married at Gretna Green, in Scotland, John Rydings of Stocks, to Miss Haighton, of this town." Why the pair should have travelled so far for the purpose is not known, and the mystery is enhanced by two facts. The pair were re-married at the Collegiate Church on September 14th of the same year; and on August 8th of the same year a marriage settlement had been duly arranged and signed between the contracting parties and their friends. In the settlement mention is made of certain properties in or near St. Mary's Gate, which had been purchased by an earlier John Rydings in 1704. John Rydings died in 1807 and was probably buried at St. Ann's Church, although in his will he directed that he should be interred in Lord Derby's Chapel in the Collegiate Church. He held Stocks and an adjacent estate called Peel under lease from Lord Derby. The extent of the two was about 35 acres. In 1805 the death occurred at Stocks of Major T. Wilkinson, of the Manchester Volunteer Infantry, but it is not recorded what relationship he bore to the Rydings family. Leaving them we pass on to a more recent tenant of Stocks.

GILBERT WINTER.

Seventy years ago Gilbert Winter lived at Stocks. He was a well-known citizen of those days, and in 1822 occupied the position of borough reeve. He carried on business as a wine merchant in an old building in St. Ann's Street. It was known as Winter's Buildings, but the name was probably given to it by Mr. Winter, for the style in which it was built suggested the idea that it was at least a century old when it was pulled down in 1878. Mr. Winter was one of the directors of the Liverpool and Manchester Railway, and the first of the meetings of the directors was held in the St. Ann's Street office of Mr. Winter. The two Stephensons, father and son, were often seen there, and many important conferences with reference to the great undertaking took place there. Mr. Winter is more notable for another association. He was extremely hospitable, and many well-known figures in literary and art circles met from time to time under his roof at Stocks.

In the early part of January, 1839, Charles Dickens and John Foster, the biographer of the novelist, visited Manchester in company with W. Harrison Ainsworth, who had left Manchester and settled down in London. The friends attended service at the Collegiate Church, where service was conducted by the Rev. R. Parkinson, the author of *The Old Church Clock*, who referred to a terrific storm that had swept over the city a few days before. The most notable incident of the visit was a dinner given in honour of the trio by Mr. Winter at Stocks. Included amongst the guests who met them were the brothers Grant, whose personality impressed itself so strongly on the mind of Dickens that within a few weeks he immortalised them as the Cheeryble Brothers in his novel *Nicholas Nickleby*, on which he was at the time engaged. We are told that on the occasion of another dinner party a little incident took place which gave rise to one of those happy impromptu speeches in which Dickens was unsurpassed. The dinner table was triangular, the room was rather small, and the host on the occasion was James Crossley, who occupied a somewhat uncomfortable position at the table sitting at the apex of the triangle with his back against the wall. Even then Mr. Crossley was stout in figure, and this, together with his position at the table attracted Mr. Dickens' attention. In proposing the host's health the great novelist remarked that "during the whole evening, seeing the peculiar position their host occupied at the dinner table, he could not help being reminded of Dr. Primrose's famous family picture in *The Vicar of Wakefield*, and he had been wondering all night however he should be got out, but was more amazed how he ever got in."

This reference to the great Manchester bibliophile reminds me that Mr. Crossley himself was the last, and perhaps the most notable resident at Stocks; and I cannot close this chapter better than by giving some account of the well-known, one-time President of the "Chetham Society."

JAMES CROSSLEY.

James Crossley, the son of a merchant, was born at the Mount, Halifax, on March 31st, 1800. His father was a man of literary tastes and a book collector, in both of which respects he was followed by his son. After receiving a course of education at Queen Elizabeth's Free Grammar School at Skircoat, Halifax, he was articled to Thomas Ainsworth, father of the novelist, whose office was in Essex Street, Manchester. Mr. Ainsworth's business was largely connected with the proposed improvements in Manchester, in the widening of Market Street, the building of a new Blackfriar's Bridge, etc. Mr. Crossley in this way was very intimately concerned in the metamorphosis that the city underwent from 1825 onwards, and in later years retained interesting memories of the town as it was in the twenties of the last century. He also made the acquaintance of his employer's eldest son, whose success in the world of letters was a matter of intense gratification to him. Another acquaintance of those early days was John Partington Aston, who after being articled to Mr. Ainsworth, entered the employment of Mr. Crossley. The three friends had a common interest in literature.

Mr. Crossley's first appearance in the world of literature was in *Blackwood*, to which he contributed a number of articles on various subjects. One was on "The Chetham Library," and another was entitled "Manchester Poetry." Early in life he was an admirer of the works of Sir Thomas Browne, and in 1822 he published through Messrs. Blackwood a small volume bearing the title, "Tracts by Sir Thomas Browne, Knight, M.D." The book was published anonymously, the "advertisement" or preface being signed "J.C." In the closing sentence of the preface he says, "To those who are admirers of Browne, it may be perhaps interesting in some measure to be informed that a full and a correct life of that singular author is preparing from ample materials, and will shortly be presented to the public." So far as Mr. Crossley was concerned, the promised life of Browne never appeared. Why, can, only be conjectured, because he continued to be an admirer of the Norwich doctor. Another student took up the work, and in 1835 Samuel Wilkins published a life together with a new edition of the complete works of Thomas Browne. One item in that book possesses special interest. It is in volume iv. and on page 273 of that volume; and bears the title of a "Fragment on Mummies." In a note Mr. Wilkins says: "From a copy in the handwriting of J. Crossley, Esq. I have given the fragment on the authority of Mr. Crossley, but have not been able to find the volume in the British Museum which contained it, nor could he inform me; having transcribed it himself, but omitted to note the volume in which he met with it." When a later edition of Wilkin's book was published in 1852 the "Fragment" was omitted; not has any person up to the present reported having seen the source from which Mr. Crossley is said to have obtained it. The mystery has never been satisfactorily cleared up, but it seems pretty certain that for some reason or other Mr. Crossley wrote the "Fragment" in the style of Browne, and sent it to Wilkins, who accepted it in the guarded fashion shown in the footnote just quoted. The only reason for Mr. Crossley's action could have been a certain amount of annoyance arising from the fact that someone else had superseded him in his contemplated work. Whether this was so or not, he so thoroughly copied the style as to mislead many persons besides Wilkins. As recently as 1886 Alexander Ireland, writing in the *City News*, recommending the study of Browne, quoted an extract from the "Fragment" as illustrative of his style; and in a letter I received from him a few days later in reply to one I had sent him, he said: "I believe the passage to be by Browne, from internal evidence alone. No man of this century could have written it." And there the matter rests.

Another curious act of Mr. Crossley's has been already referred to in a previous volume. In 1840 Rivington's, of London, published a new edition of Wallis's *Lectures on the Trinity*, with the name of "T. Flintoff" on the title-page as editor. In Mr. Crossley's own copy, which I possess, he explains how it came about that his friend's name appeared on the title-page instead of his own.

Strange though it may appear to us, Mr. Crossley was strongly opposed to the incorporation of Manchester, and took a prominent part in the fight against the proposal. On the other hand literary and educational movements found in him an ardent supporter. He was one of the committee who organised the first Manchester Musical Festival in 1828. He took an active part in the work of the early years of the Manchester Athenæum, and was President of the institution for three years; and took part in the establishment of the Free Library in 1852.

But perhaps, apart from his personality and his industry as a book collector (for he amassed a collection of 60,000 volumes) he was best known in connection with the Chetham Society, of which he was the founder. The Society originated with a group of literary friends who met in 1843 at Mr. Crossley's house in Booth Street, Piccadilly. Dr. Edward Holme was elected first President, an office he continued to hold until his death in 1848, when Mr. Crossley was chosen to succeed him. Until his death, in 1883, Mr. Crossley held the office; and so keen was his interest in the work of the Society that until his death he was never absent from the annual meeting of the members. His interest in the Chetham Hospital and Library was just as keen as it was in the Society, and in March, 1875, the governors of the institution resolved that in acknowledgement of the services Mr. Crossley had rendered for many years his portrait should be painted and placed in the library. A subscription list was opened, Mr. J. H. Walker was commissioned to paint the portrait, and on October 4th, 1875 it was formally presented to the governors, along with an album containing the signatures of the subscribers, which was presented to Mr. Crossley. Mr. Crossley was a member of many literary societies, amongst which were the Spencer Society, the Cambden Society, the English Dialect Society, and the Library Association of the United Kingdom.

He lived for forty years at Booth Street, Piccadilly, after which he removed to a large house in Cavendish Street, All Saints. When those premises were required for business purposes he removed to Stocks House where he died. The work that he did for the Chetham and other Societies was very great; for in addition to preparing a number of volumes on a variety of subjects, he assisted in the revision of most of the volumes published by them. This entailed an enormous amount of labour which was always cheerfully given.

Needless to say Mr. Crossley's position in the literary world brought him in contact with the leading literary characters of over half a century. Indeed, it may be said that hardly a single writer of note existed in the country who had not in some way or other come in contact with him. In this connection his reminiscences were extremely interesting. Professional engagements frequently took him to London, and in his earlier years he stayed at the Old Hummums Hotel in Covent Garden. Many were the pleasant reunions connected with those visits, some of them being summarised in the following sentence: "Now a little supper with Talfourd and Maclise at the Garrick; anon a visit to Bulwer at Knebworth; a breakfast with Disraeli; a chop with John Forster in Lincoln's Inn Fields; a snug little dinner with Dickens in Devonshire Terrace; or a gathering at Ainsworth's house at Kersal, on the Harrow Road." He had met Charles Lamb, and William Godwin, William Hazlitt and Leigh Hunt, Basil Montagu and George Dyer, Coleridge and Thomas de Quincey.

As an after-dinner speaker he was almost without a peer; and as a conversationalist his style was reminiscent of Dr. Johnson. In him were combined elegant tastes, a refined courtesy of manner, and a uniform kindness in communicating to others the treasures of a well stored mind and an extensive knowledge of books. He died at the advanced age of 83, and his remains were interred at St. Paul's Church, Kersal. His funeral was attended by a large number of representative men including deputations from many learned societies and public institutions.

Mr. Crossley was never married. For several generations he was one of the most familiar figures in Manchester Streets; and to many who were not personally acquainted with him his kindly, quaint face, surmounted by a broad brimmed silk hat from under which strayed his venerable white hair, was well known. He was one of the last of the book lovers of our city who systematically haunted the book stalls, examining with a keen eye their contents, and bidding down the price asked by the stall keeper for some volume or volumes. This bidding down was a well-known feature of "Old Crossley," as he was called by booksellers and stall keepers; and it was said by some who knew him well that he was never known to pay the price originally asked for a second-hand book. It was that custom of running down of prices that caused him to miss a *Wynkyn de Worde*, now to be found amongst the treasures in our Reference Library. The book, after lying upon Johnson's stall in Corporation Street, was bought by Bob Holt and placed upon his stall. Mr. Crossley saw the volume, which was apparently a copy of *Holinshed's Chronicles*, but with which had been bound a copy of the rarer volume. After much chaffering on the part of the would-be purchaser the true nature of the volume was accidentally discovered by another person; and as a result it was generously given by Holt to the Reference Library. After Mr. Crossley's death his vast collection of books was sold by auction, and Stocks House, once again without a tenant, remained empty for some time. After a few years it was pulled down, and the most interesting building in the neighbourhood was lost.

CHEETHAM HILL ROAD AND CHEETHAM HILL.

PART IV.

SOME PLACES OF WORSHIP.

ST. MARK'S CHURCH.

When our forefathers of the closing decades of the eighteenth century erected places of worship they often paid no heed to architectural considerations. Providing that a sufficiently seating accommodation was supplied, no other consideration seemed to be considered. Plain red bricks, unrelieved by stone work, severe simplicity of style, and internally high backed, straight backed pews were the leading features of most of the places of worship erected from 1790 to 1820.

The first such building in Cheetham Hill was built quite in accordance with these ideas. It was of red brick, was innocent of architectural beauty, and was large enough to accommodate about a thousand persons. It owed its origin to the generosity of the Rev. E. Ethelstone, but was finished by his son, the Rev. C. W. Ethelstone, who was a fellow of the Collegiate Church. The latter was born in Manchester in 1767, was the first Minister of St. Mark's, and held the position until his death on September 14th, 1830. He was a man of literary tastes, and wrote a volume of poems. During the excitement that overspread the country at the beginning of the last century, the Manchester and Salford corps of Volunteers was formed. Mr. Ethelstone was appointed Chaplain to the corps, and he consecrated their colours at the Collegiate Church. As a preacher he was popular, a fine voice and good delivery being important factors to this end. The church having been built as a chapel of ease to the Collegiate Church the service was a plain one, the clerk taking the place of the choir in many cases. One story of the parson and clerk is worthy of repetition. " Philip, the clerk, was a character, and in a thin, wiry voice he led the responses, assisted by the richer tones of some few of the elders of the congregation. He was not a man of great erudition, and he studied the even verses of the Psalms which fell to his portion, but from bad sight and absence of study he was not up in the odd verses. One Sunday, by accident, Mr. Ethelstone omitted a verse, in fact, read Philip's own verse. In vain he waited for Philip. That worthy functionary made no response—he would not venture upon an odd verse. Mr. Ethelstone still paused, but Philip gave sundry kicks in his desk, coughed, and cleared up, as if he had a bad cough—all to gain time. Mr. Ethelstone then read another verse, but unfortunately he again made 'a false quantity' and read another even verse. No response from Philip. Mr. Ethelstone leaned over and said in audible tones: 'The fifteenth verse.' Still no voice from Philip. Then the preacher in despair read fortunately the fifteenth verse, and prepared to go through the whole Psalm, thinking

Philip was taken ill, when at the end of the verse both parson and clerk struck in for the sixteenth verse, and both read through it, Philip finishing first. After this the two readers fell into their proper places.

It is said also of Philip, that being very much addicted to tobacco chewing; he would often remove a quid from his mouth at certain parts of the service, place it on his desk, but would take it up again later on. The Church was not consecrated until 1839, and was not made the centre of a parish until 1850. Under the late G. W. Reynolds, who was the Secretary of the Diocesan Church Building Society, the seats were made free. Mr. Ethelstone had as his curate for some years the Rev. Peter Hordern, who had been Librarian at the Chetham Library from 1821 to 1834. One of Mr. Hordern's daughters married Sir John Lubbock, Bart., M.P., and became Lady Ellen Frances Lubbock.

ST. LUKE'S CHURCH.

St. Luke's Church was built by public subscription in 1836, the site being given by the Earl of Derby. The architect was Mr. T. W. Alkinson, the cost of erection exceeding £23,000. The schools which stand near to the principal entrance to the churchyard were built in 1844 at a cost of £1,000. The first rector of St. Luke's was the Rev. John Chippendall, whose father had contributed a thousand pounds towards the cost of building. Mr. Chippendall was rector for nearly forty years. The most noteworthy incident in the history of the church is the fact that in 1847 Mendelssohn visited it and played upon the organ, a fine instrument built by Hill. The great musician-composer first conducted a performance of his oratorio "Elijah" at the Birmingham Musical Festival of 1846, and in the following year he visited Manchester to conduct another performance of the same oratorio, and during the visit was taken to see the new organ in St. Luke's Church upon which he performed. He died on November 4th, 1847. For several generations the churchyard has been well-known as a place for interment, and within its boundaries are gathered the mortal remains of many of Manchester's best-known citizens. All branches of science, art and literature together with social reform, municipal effort, and philanthropy are represented on the headstones that record the last memories of the dead.

WESLEYAN METHODIST CHAPELS.

About a century ago the first services in connection with Wesleyan Methodism held in the village took place under primitive conditions. As the visitor passes the two fine chapels that now accommodate the Wesleyan Methodist section of the population, he can with difficulty realise that a century ago a kitchen in a private house provided sufficient accommodation for the persons who were desirous of attending the services. The first meeting was the kitchen of Mr. Samuel Russell's house; and when the accommodation thus provided proved to be too limited, he built a room over his coachhouse. This served for a few years, when a chapel was built which was opened in 1817 by Dr. Adam Clarke. For twenty years services were held in the little chapel, when, in 1837, a more imposing structure was erected. Since then the old chapel has been used as a mortuary chapel in connection with the cemetery, where so many leading Wesleyans of the last seventy years have been buried. In more recent time the Victoria Wesleyan Chapel has been built, and last year a new building has superseded the Chapel built in 1837. The Cheetham Chapel was made the centre of a new circuit in 1863, since when a further change has been made by the formation of the Victoria circuit. The growth of Wesleyan Methodism in the Cheetham Hill district in the course of a century is illustrated by the fact that the small group of people who met in the little room over the coach-house is represented to-day by the congregations that meet in the thirteen chapels that form the Cheetham Hill and Victoria circuits.

ST. CHAD'S ROMAN CATHOLIC CHAPEL.

Like many other places of worship in our city, St. Chad's is one of a series that have succeeded each other as the town has extended its borders. It is believed to be in direct succession from the temporary chapel that, in the days of persecution, was located on the bank of the river near to Blackfriar's Bridge. Services were there conducted in secret, sentinels being stationed upon the stairs in Parsonage to give warning in case the pursuivants or priest-hunters made their appearance. Under better conditions the congregation removed to the little building off Church Street, the site of which is denoted by Roman Entry that formerly gave access to the chapel. In 1774 a move was made to a larger building in Rook Street. For over seventy years services were held at Rook Street; but in 1847 a further change was made. The old building was abandoned and was afterwards converted into business premises, forming part of the warehouse occupied for many years by Messrs. S. Ogden & Co. One who remembers the chapel says that its outer aspect was that of an exaggerated three storied weaving shop of an old fashioned type. Unassuming as the building was in appearance, some distinguished ecclesiastics visited it. They included Cardinal Manning, then plain Dr. Manning; Dr. Ullathorne; Cardinal Wiseman, then Father Nicholas Wiseman; and the Rev. George Spencer, brother to Lord Althorp. In 1847 the new chapel in Cheetham Hill Road was opened, and was consecrated by Dr. Brown, Vicar Apostolic of the Lancashire district. The altar in the Lady Chapel was consecrated by Dr. Briggs, Vicar Apostolic of the Yorkshire district. The ceremony took place on August 3rd, and was attended by sixty Roman Catholic clergymen. Amongst the many who have officiated at St. Chad's during the sixty years of its existence, perhaps the best known was the late Right Rev. Monsignor Gadd—who afterwards became Vicar General.

SOME JEWISH PLACES OF WORSHIP.

In my last volume I gave the story of the growth of the congregation attending the Great Synagogue, and in doing so, referred to the fact that about a century ago the Jewish population of the city was to be found in the neighbourhood of Long Millgate, where for so many years their only place of worship in Manchester was situated. Since then a change has taken place and roughly speaking the Jewish area may be described as lying between Strangeways and Cheetham Hill Road, together with those thoroughfares and the streets running off them. Reference has been made to the Great Synagogue, the foundation stone of which was laid in 1857. The building was consecrated on March 25th, 1858. Philip Dessen, who had officiated at Halliwell Street for about seven years, was appointed first reader, with S. H. Simonson, a profound scholar, as second reader. A fortnight before the building was consecrated, the foundation stone of another synagogue was laid. The site chosen was at the corner of York Street (now Cheetham Hill Road) and Park Street, and the name of the "Congregation of British Jews" was adopted. The first minister was the Rev. Dr. Solomon M. Schiller-Szinessy, a Hungarian by descent. He was followed by another profound scholar, Dr. Gottheill, who was succeeded in 1874 by Dr. Wienner. The best-known minister connected with the Great Synagogue was the Rev. Professor David Meyer Isaacs, who for nearly twenty years was regarded as the ablest among the Anglo-Jewish preachers of his day.

From 1850 to 1880 there was a great increase in the numbers of the Jewish settlement by reason of a number of Spanish, Portugese, Syrian, and Corfu merchants who in their dealings with Constantinople, Salonica, Alexandria, Cairo, Beyront, and most of the Levant markets monopolised much ground previously held by British and Greek merchants. One of their number interested himself very actively in the matter of providing another place of worship that should meet the case created by the accession of these new-comers. As a result the "Spanish and Portugese

Synagogue" was built in Cheetham Hill Road and was opened in 1874.

A number of other places of worship have been opened in and around Cheetham Hill Road in the course of the last forty years, but there is little of general interest to record concerning them.

CHEETHAM HILL AND CHEETHAM HILL ROAD.

PART V.

HALLIWELL LANE AND SMEDLEY LANE.

HALLIWELL LANE.

Halliwell Lane was, rather more than a century ago, nothing more than a cartway used by farmers for gaining access to certain of their fields; and so it remained until James Halliwell interested himself in the matter of making it a public thoroughfare. Mr. Halliwell was partner in the Manchester firm of Peel, Greaves & Co., and like the first Sir Robert Peel, came from Bury. Soon after settling down in Manchester, about 1788, he bought land in Cheetham Hill and built a mansion which he called Broomfield. It stood in finely laid out grounds behind the bowling green attached to the Griffin Inn, and was approached from Halliwell Lane. Seventy years ago Halliwell Lane was pretty much as Mr. Halliwell had left it. Passing along it from the main road there were a few houses on both sides; Falcon Villa on the right hand, with Lane Villa and two terraces named Marshall Place and Halliwell Place just beyond, on the left. Then there were fields and gardens until the approach to Broomfield on the right with Ash Lodge on the opposite side were passed. Some distance further on, on the right, after the bend in the lane had been passed, was another mansion, Oak Hill, but this was the only other house until Tetlow Lane was reached. Then along Tetlow Lane and down Northumberland Street only about four houses were passed after leaving Oak Hill. Such was a rural walk opened out through the influence of James Halliwell.

Halliwell was in some respects a remarkable man. He was brought up in a factory, but he displayed such energy and force of character that his employer took an interest in him. He had extraordinary aptitude for business, and was good at figures and mental arithmetic; but had no taste for reading, and was in many respects very much behind as a scholar. A very funny story is told concerning Mr. Halliwell that is too good to pass by. On one occasion he sent a present to a friend in London who, in acknowledging the receipt of it, said that he hoped to send an equivalent shortly. The word "equivalent" was a new one to the unlettered business man, who made it out to mean an elephant. He accordingly had a high wall built round a small field behind his house, and was preparing to built a suitable house, when a friend, seeing the preparations, asked the purport of them. A few words sufficed to show Mr. Halliwell how thoroughly he had misunderstood his correspondent's letter, and both friends had a hearty laugh about it. The story being told "on Change" many inquiries were made concerning the mysterious present, and Mr. Halliwell was the object for plenty of chaff amongst his business friends. He died in 1807 aged sixty-two years.

One of the earlier residents in Halliwell Lane was

William Shore, who for over thirty years was organist at Cross Street Chapel; and who was well-known in his day as a musical composer. He along with a group of fellow musical enthusiasts commenced the Gentlemen's Glee Club in 1830. He presided at the first concert given by the Club at the York Hotel, King Street, on September 8th, 1830, and was elected honorary member the following year. He was honorary secretary in 1833 and on several occasions acted as conductor. In the list of glees, etc. performed at the meetings of the Club are included six pieces composed by Mr. Shore; and to one of them, a glee, "Come, Sweet Mirth," was awarded a prize in 1831. Mr. Shore was also a founder of the Manchester Madrigal Society, and was a member of the committee who arranged the last Choral Festival held in the Collegiate Church in 1830. He died at Buxton in 1877, aged 86 years. Another resident was David Ainsworth, manufacturer, who was borough reeve in 1840.

SMEDLEY LANE.

Although Smedley Lane retains a certain amount of semi-rural appearance, things were very different there when St. Luke's Church was built. Behind the church, standing in the midst of fields was Smedley Cottage, and a little distance beyond on the same side was Beech Hill. Between the grounds of Beech Hill and those of Smedley Hill was a farmers' road leading into the fields now represented by a paved street, Smedley Road was a private road and near to the end of it was Smedley Old Hall with the New Hall in the immediate neighbourhood. On the opposite side of Smedley Lane some of the old fashioned residences still standing were pleasantly situated, open fields extending in front as far as Collyhurst. The last house on that side of the lane was Smedley Bank, which stood nearly opposite to Beech Hill. Queen's Road was a country lane known by the curious name of "Job's Stile-path," and at the corner of Smedley Road and the lane stood Merryfield House, the residence of Mr. Longworth, whose daughter played so important a part in the celebrated Yelverton case. Just below Merryfield House were the Arcade Gardens, a pleasure resort where boating and fishing could be enjoyed. The gardens joined up to the New Hall grounds. In a book entitled *Bowling and Bowling Greens*, published in 1876, the author, Robert Wood, makes an interesting reference to the Old Hall. He says: "At Smedley Old Hall in the township of, Cheetham, there is a curious old bowling green in connection with a series of terraces well worth the attention of the archæologist and the antiquary. The place is believed to have been the original headquarters of the Chetham family, and there has perhaps been a Smedley Hall of some kind for eight hundred or a thousand years. It appears to me that the level ground, now made into a garden, was once used as a tilting ground, and the terraces were made for the spectators. The terraces are cut out of the hill side, three feet deep, and nearly two hundred yards long; near the centre of which is a still more elevated mound, projecting forward, and overlooking all the other terraces. This may have been constructed for the Queen of Beauty and her lady attendants, who could not only see everything going on upon the tilting ground and terraces, but would be ready to applaud and crown the victors.

At the end nearest the Hall the top terrace has been cut back to make room for the bowling green, and continued so as to enclose it on two sides, to form an elevated platform for the friends of the family and visitors to occupy when watching the bowlers. But the age of chivalry is past; the level ground and the terraces are now being made into an Italian garden, and the bowling green is chiefly used as a croquet ground. Everything gives way to progress."

Reference has been made to James Chetham who lived at Smedley Hall. On the death of Edward Chetham in 1769 his estates were divided between his sisters Alice, who married Adam Bland, and Mary, who married Samuel of Clowes, of Broughton Hall.

Smedley Cottage was a old fashioned house that stood at the corner of Johnson Street and Smedley Lane. Before the district was built up as it is to-day Smedley Cottage was a pleasant place to live in. In its garden and orchard were fine fruit trees that bore many great crops of apples, pears, plums and cherries. There was also a fountain and fish pond, together with poultry yard, pig styes, and stables. Johnson Street was so named by George Johnson, who lived at Smedley Cottage, and who engaged in a law suit with "Lord" Statter, as he was called, agent for Lord Derby as to a right of way into "Job's Stile-path." Mr. Johnson won the day, but at a cost of over £2,000. He was somewhat noted as an owner of race horses, and from time to time had some well-known animals stabled at

Smedley Lane. Perhaps the most notable of these was Jupiter, with which he won the Liverpool Cup many years ago.

When George Johnson left Cheetham Hill, and went to live at Bucklow Hill, his brother, John, took up residence at the Cottage. He was partner with the late Alderman Harry Rawson in the printing firm of Johnson & Rawson.

The cottage and stables were pulled down about thirty years ago, and the site together with the garden was covered with houses and shops. The houses in Luke Street, and a row of houses and shops in Smedley Lane now occupy the ground, the Post Office being on the site of the Cottage.

Smedley Bank is principally notable as having been the residence of the Rev. Canon Wray, who died there in 1866. Cecil Daniel Wray was born at Doncaster in 1778, and after graduating at Oxford, occupied several curacies until 1809, when he was appointed Clerk in Orders of the Collegiate Church of Manchester. In his *Early Recollections of the Collegiate Church, Manchester* he gives some interesting particulars regarding the conduct of services there a century ago. He says in one place: "When I first came to Manchester in 1809, the Sunday morning lecture always commenced in the nave at six o'clock. The first bell tolled at five, then at half past five; at six o'clock Mr. Brookes or myself were always in the reading desk, ready to begin the Litany." The attendance at those early morning services ranged from 200 to 300 persons. Until his death Canon Wray remained associated with the Cathedral. He was an aggressive

Churchman and was largely responsible for the movement that resulted in the erection of St. Andrew's Church, Ancoats; St. Matthew's, Campfield; St. George's, Hulme, and St. Philip's, Salford. When Miss Atherton contemplated building Holy Trinity Church, Hulme, Mr. Wray was the first person consulted by her. In 1847, whilst preaching the anniversary sermon of the Chetham Hospital, he called attention to the fact that no memorial of the founder existed. As a result of this George Pilkington saw Mr. Wray after the service, and offered £200, or as much as would be necessary to supply a statue. The outcome was the fine monument by Theed in the Cathedral and the memorial windows. Canon Wray took a prominent part in promoting the "Ten Hours Bill," and was often seen on public platforms in company with the Earl of Shaftesbury, Lord John Manners, and other leaders of the movement. His services to the Sunday School movement was recognised by paving the chancel of the Cathedral with encaustic tiles in 1859, at the close of his fifty years of service. He founded the "Canon Wray's Birthday Gift," a charity distributed annually on his birthday by the Minor Canons. It takes the form of good worsted stockings for eight poor men and eight poor women, the figures representing 88, his age in 1865, when he founded the charity. He died on April 27th, 1866, and was interred in the Cathedral churchyard.

In 1836 John Rylands resided in Smedley Lane, and he had as a near neighbour Eustratio Ralli, merchant founder of the well-known firm of that name, whose warehouse at that time was at 13 Parsonage.

CHEETHAM HILL AND CHEETHAM HILL ROAD.

PART VI.

SOME WELL-KNOWN RESIDENTS.

GEORGE WILSON.

When Manchester was incorporated, George Wilson who carried on business as a starch manufacturer and who resided at Moreton Street, Cheetham, was returned as one of the first councillors for St. Michael's Ward. He only continued to hold a seat in the Council until 1842 when he resigned. But although his career in the municipal council was of such brief duration, his services to Manchester and the commerce of the country were such as to merit special reference. Mr. Wilson was born in April, 1808, at Hathersage, in Derbyshire, where his father carried on business as a corn miller. In 1813 the family removed to Manchester; and in due course George was apprenticed to a corn merchant in Manchester. As a young man he commenced travelling on behalf of his employer, and in that way picked up a variety of information respecting the conditions of labour and the position of the workers that served him in good stead in after years. As a young man he engaged in many movements for reform, and soon realised that the Reform Bill of 1832 would not yield the results that some of the extreme Radicals had anticipated would follow its adoption. He saw that the causes of the poverty and suffering then general amongst the working classes lay deeper than many had anticipated, and realised that the only way in which to secure prosperity and contentment in the country was to remove the fetters that tied down the commerce of the country, and prevented the free inflow of food into the country. At the time that these views were forming themselves in his mind the proposal for the corporation of the town was first made, and met with strong opposition. Mr. Wilson, however, took up the matter with determination and enthusiasm, and although splendid services were rendered by Richard Çobden, Joseph Heron, and others, it was owing to his powers of organisation that success was achieved with comparative ease. His services in the cause were acknowledged by a number of his fellow townsmen, who presented him with a costly gold watch, which he wore to the day of his death.

When the provisional committee, out of which arose the Anti Corn Law Association, was formed, Mr. Wilson was included, and he attended all the preliminary meetings. At a meeting of the council of the League held on April 13th, 1839, he was elected Chairman, and he retained the position until the dissolution of the League in 1846. For seven years he gave his life almost exculsively to the movement, and to give an epitome of his services would be to write a history of the League. His election to the responsible position of Chairman was owing to the efforts of Mr. Cobden, who had noted Mr. Wilson's great powers as an organiser, and his possession of controlling ability and tact in an almost unexampled degree. Mr. Cobden's judgment proved to be sound, and it was often said of his nominee in after years that he was "born a chairman." As the work of the League increased the demands upon the Chairman increased, but he never swerved nor showed signs of flagging interest in the work. He was always calm and deliberate in the conduct of meetings, and it mattered little whether it was a small sub-committee that he was presiding over or a densely crowded public meeting, his demeanour was ever the same. He was practically the originator in later years of the National Reform Union, and to his death continued to be an active worker in connection with it. Some idea of the amount of energy that he put into his work will be realised from the fact that during the winter of 1866–7 he attended over two hundred meetings in connection with the Union. In another direction Mr. Wilson rendered valuable aid to several great commercial undertakings. He was associated with Mr. Ricardo in establishing the Electric Telegraph Company, and was the first person to conceive the idea of telegraphing public news, and in 1847 he put his idea into operation. The Manchester to Leeds wires were in the process of laying when Mr. Cobden was nominated for the West Riding of Yorkshire. Mr. Wilson, who was a director of the Company, had several miles of wire carried temporarily to Wakefield, and from that town the proceedings attendant on the nomination and election of Mr. Cobden were telegraphed to Manchester, and appeared in a second edition of the *Manchester Times* about two o'clock the same day. This was the first telegraphic newspaper report on record.

About the same time Mr. Wilson was elected a director of the Lancashire and Yorkshire Railway Company, and in July, 1847, he was elected vice-chairman, which position he afterwards resigned. In 1860 he was elected deputy-chairman, and retained the position until his death. He was the means of starting the Night Asylum. During the terrible winter of 1842 several persons died in the streets of the town, and as a result Mr. Wilson, along with Mr. Joseph Adshead, "Manchester's Man of Ross," opened a subscription list to provide shelter for the poor homeless wanderers of the night. In this way originated the Night Asylum. In many other ways Mr. Wilson rendered valuable services to Manchester, and it was therefore not surprising that his death should have been the cause for sorrow on the part of thousands of his fellow townsmen. His death was sudden. On December 29th, 1870, he left Manchester by the nine o'clock express to Liverpool on railway business. After the train had passed Wigan he complained to a friend of being ill, and before Liverpool was reached he was dead. He was buried at the Ardwick cemetery.

JOHN HARLAND, F.S.A.

Another well-known resident of the Cheetham Hill district was John Harland, who formerly lived at Brideoak Street. Mr. Harland was a native of Hull, where he was born in 1806. He learned the trade of a letterpress printer, but, being of a literary turn, he prepared himself for more important labours. Studying shorthand, he became one of the most expert writers in shorthand in the country. In 1830 he came to Manchester to take up a position in connection with the *Manchester Guardian*. As a reporter Mr. Harland had to contend with many difficulties unknown to the journalist of to-day. Many of his reports were written while travelling in a stage-coach; and it was frequently said that the details of a trial at Lancaster assizes were printed in the *Guardian* before the judge and jury had recovered from the labours of the court. On one occasion, Mr. Harland's powers were put to a remarkable test. A man was being tried at Lancaster for making a seditious speech, and Mr. Harland had to produce and read his notes as evidence against him. These notes were read slowly to allow the judge to write down the evidence. While this was going on the counsel for the defence turned to a gentleman near him, and said: "I'll turn this fellow inside out." The cross-examination for the defence began: "You profess to give the exact words?"

"Yes!"

"You say the prisoner said so-and-so; now read what immediately follows."

Mr. Harland turned to the place in his notes, and read off without hesitation, and without waiting for his evidence to be taken down, a passage of about a hundred words. Again he was required to turn to another part of the speech, and the second passage thus read agreed perfectly with what the counsel knew the prisoner had said. The learned counsel desisted, and remarked to the gentlemen to whom he had previously spoken : "I don't think there's another man in England could do that."

Mr. Harland was, in fact, the father of provincial reporting. In 1836 the *Guardian* from being a weekly became a bi-weekly publication, and in 1855 the daily issue commenced ; and in the meantime Mr. Harland had advanced from the position of reporter to that of editor. In the last named capacity he drew around him some of the most able journalists of the time. Under his guidance the *Guardian* rose to a high position among the journals of the day, and to a great extent the position that the newspaper holds to-day is owing to the efforts made and the ability displayed forty and fifty years ago by its former editor. Mr. Harland did not confine his efforts to newspaper work. He was a fine Latin scholar, was well acquainted with early English history, and made a special study of ancient manuscripts and inscriptions. His contributions on antiquarian subjects to the columns of his newspaper, led to his election as a Fellow of the Society of Antiquaries. He was a very active member of the Chetham Society, for which he edited or compiled fourteen volumes in thirteen years. These included *The House and Farm Accounts of the Shuttleworths of Gawthorpe Hall*; *The Lancashire Lieutenancy under the Tudors and Stuarts* : *Mamecestre, Chapters from the early recorded History of the Barony, etc. of Manchester* : *The Court Leet Records of the Manor of Manchester in the 16th Century* : *Collectanea relating to Manchester and its Neighbourhood* : and *Three Lancashire Documents of the 14th and 15th Centuries*. In addition to these Mr. Harland published *The Autobiography of William Stout, a Lancashire Quaker: A Memoir of Sawley Abbey; Lancashire Lyrics; Ballads and Songs of Lancashire*, and in conjunction with T. T. Wilkinson, a volume of *Lancashire Folk-Lore*. As though these undertakings were not sufficient he edited a new issue of Baines's *Lancashire*, a labour which involved the re-writing of nearly the whole book. At the time of his death he contemplated a new edition of *Gregson's Fragments*.

As will be gathered from the foregoing list, Mr. Harland was a tireless worker, and he has left, as permanent records of his industry, books that will be appreciated by all who take an interest in the history of our city and county for many generations to come. He died on April 23rd, 1868, and was interred at Rusholme Road Cemetery.

Mr. Harland was one of the original members of the brotherhood of Rosicrucians, who devoted much time to antiquarian research. The Rosicrucians were a number of gentlemen who adopted the title of "The Order of Rosicrucians or Brotherhood of the Holy Cross." The original members comprised N. Gardner, Superintendent Registrar of Deaths; T. Jones, B.A., Librarian of Chetham's College; Dr. Joseph Jordan; J. Just; W. Langton, who designed a heading for the circular summoning a meeting of the Brotherhood; John Leigh, afterwards first Medical Officer of Health for the city; Dr. Frank Renand; W. W. Whitaker, and J. Harland. As vacancies arose honorary members were promoted to full membership. The transactions of the Society were published in the *Guardian*.

E. W. BINNEY, F.R.S., F.G.S.

Mr. E. W. Binney was born in 1812 at Morton, in Nottinghamshire, and served his articles with a solicitor at Chesterfield. He came to Manchester in 1836 and resided for some time in the house in Brideoak Street occupied later by Mr. John Harland. As a solicitor he had the conduct of the case of the successful claimant in the great Chadwick lawsuit of 1842.

It was, however, rather as a scientist that Mr. Binney demands attention. Geology soon found in him an attentive student, and every hour that could be snatched from professional duties was devoted to the study of his favourite branch of science. He assisted in the foundation of the Manchester Geological Society in 1838, and was a liberal contributor to its museum. In 1842 he was elected a member of the Literary and Philosophical Society, and at the time of his death he occupied the presidential chair. In his early Manchester days Mr. Binney made the acquaintance of the members of the Prestwich Botanical Society, and attended some of the Sunday meetings of the members. In this way he met Buxton, Crowther, Horsefield, Mellor, and other notable Lancashire artizan naturalists of the day. When' Richard Buxton (who lived at 72 Gun Street, Ancoats) published his *Botanical Guide* in 1849 he received very considerable assistance from Mr. Binney, who also wrote the sketch of Manchester geology prefixed to the volume. He was President of the Manchester Botanists' Association for a number of years, and in various ways sought to encourage the study of botany and mathematics amongst working men. He was industrious with his pen and his scientific papers, notes, and memoirs numbered nearly a hundred. Many of these were read before the members of the Literary and Philosophical Society; but others were read before the British Association, or were contributed to the publications of the Royal Society, the West Yorkshire Geological Society, the Geological Society, and other scientific bodies. He was elected a Fellow of the Geological Society in 1853, and of the Royal Society in 1856; and was honorary member of the Geological Societies of Edinburgh and Liverpool, and the Geological and Polytechnical Society of the West Riding of Yorkshire. He died at Cheetham Hill on December 19th, 1881, and was interred at Worsley.

JOHN BROOKS.

John Brooks was one of the three sons of William Brooks who came to Manchester from Blackburn more than 80 years ago. They engaged in different undertakings, Thomas joining the concern known afterwards as Grimshaw & Brooks, Samuel becoming associated with Reddish, Brooks & Co., and a few years later founding the well-known bank; and John becoming a partner; with Mr. Butterworth in the firm of Butterworth & Brooks. He was born at Whalley in 1786. As a business man he was very successful, but from various causes did not amass a fortune equal to that of his brother Samuel. He was an expert in all matters pertaining to commercial politics, and it is recorded how in 1841 he completely silenced Lord Stanley at Lancaster when questioning his lordship on the subject. His mode of speaking and of embodying his speeches with facts was original and forcible, and was strikingly characteristic of the plain bluntness and truthfulness of the man. He was one of the earliest and most zealous members of the Council of the Anti-Corn Law League, and until its dissolution was one of its hardest workers. In May, 1848, being impaired in health, by the unresting strain upon his physical and mental energies, he went for change to the United States, but returned without deriving permanent benefit, and he died at his residence at Clarendon House, Cheetham Hill, on October 27th, 1849. Although holding Conservative views, he was exceedingly tolerant of other men's opinion. In fact, liberality controlled his every action. He gave freely of his wealth in support of the political opinions he held, and was more than liberal in his reward for services rendered. At the time of his death he had a large number of pensioners. His generosity was at times imposed upon, as, for instance, in the case of a friend who seemed to have a large amount of property which he represented to be unencumbered. One morning he received the news that his creditor had failed, and that he had lost the large sum of £70,000 which he had lent him. Mr. Brooks was very much annoyed, and told his manager at the warehouse that he had been so deceived that he had resolved to cease lending and giving money. Hardly had he uttered the words than a poor woman with some ragged children made her appearance. In spite of what he had only just said he told the clerk to give her a shilling, The clerk reminded him of his resolution but he said in reply: "Well, well, but don't begin with this woman and her children." He never did begin; and it was only when death appeared that he did cease his benevolencies.

Many other well-known citizens have been associated with Cheetham Hill, including amongst them Alderman Muirhead, the founder of the well-known fish and poultry business who was born in Edinburgh, but came to Manchester early in life. He represented Collegiate Church Ward in the council from 1867 to 1879, when he was elected an Alderman. He died on February 24th, 1885.

Better known than Alderman Muirhead was Alderman Robert Neill, the contractor and builder whose success in business was remarkable. He came from Musselburgh in Scotland as a journeyman joiner in 1834. He commenced business on his own account in a very small way in Sherborne Street, and in 1858 he added a part of the property now occupied by the firm in Broughton Lane. From 1846 to 1865 he frequently assisted in the practical work connected with carrying out the important contracts he secured, but in 1865 he felt that he could abandon this practice owing to the fact that his two sons who had been trained to the business were admitted partners in the concern. The number of important buildings erected by the firm since then has been great; few firms of building contractors in England being better known. Although he spent so much of his time, thought, and energy in building up a business, Mr. Neill did not confine his efforts to commerce, but for many years took his part in the government of the city. He was elected a Councillor for Cheetham Ward in 1852 and was promoted to the Aldermanic bench in 1862, which position he resigned in 1869. He was Mayor of the city in 1866–7 and 1867–8; and during his second year of mayoralty he laid the foundation stone of the City Police Courts in Minshull Street on July 10th, and on October 26th he performed the same ceremony in connection with the new Town Hall, Albert Square. His closing years were spent in retirement in Rutlandshire.

Another resident in Cheetham Hill Road was John Grave, who joined the Council in 1856, was elected Alderman in 1862, and was Mayor from 1868 to 1871, during which period the waterworks scheme was extended, and Deansgate was widened. Reference will be made to James Croston, the writer of several interesting books relating to Lancashire topography, and to several other one-time residents of Cheetham Hill, will be made in connection with other matters.

CHEETHAM HILL AND CHEETHAM HILL ROAD.

PART VII.

HOW THE DISTRICT WAS REPRESENTED IN THE DIRECTORY FOR 1824.

In connection with some of our old directories of Manchester there was published *A List of the Merchants, Manufacturers, and Tradesmen in the Market Towns and Principal Villages within twenty-four miles of Manchester.* Cheetham Hill was included under the general heading of Middleton, along with Blackley, Broughton, Crumpsall, Harpurhey, Hopwood, Kersal Moor, Smedley and Tonge. It is interesting to glance through the short list of names that represent our district as it was in 1824.

In the first place it may be noted that the complete list comprises only sixty names. In many cases the addresses appear as Cheetham Hill only. In all such it is probable that they lived on the main road. Including these there are twenty-two entries relating to the residents on the highway, exclusive of cottages. Included in the list is E. W. Pilkington, whose bow and arrow shop was a well-known landmark for many years. We also find mention made of the licensed houses which then comprised the Robin Hood, the Bird in Hand, the Griffin, and the Eagle and Child. To three of these bowling greens were attached, that of the last-named being perhaps the best known. Robert Wood in his book on bowling greens refers to the old Eagle and Child Inn thus: "On the Cheetham Hill Road there was formerly an old hostelry or roadside public house, known as the Eagle and Child. This house was framed with timber, had projecting gables, and was altogether a picture of old age, and at last became so ruinous that about twenty five years ago (about 1851) it had to be taken down, and the present Temple Hotel was built in its place. To this house there was a bowling green attached from time immemorial, and was probably as old as the house itself, which by appearance would be nearly three hundred years old. It was on this green on the 17th of August, 1819, that Samuel Bamford and a few coadjutors lunched off cold veal and ham, a part of what should have been their previous day's dinner, if they had not been so roughly handled and dispersed by the yeomanry."

Samuel Barnes was the landlord of the inn in 1824. Near neighbours of his were the Misses Appleton, who lived at Temple Cottage, and some half dozen manufacturers whose residences are generally described as Temple. The residences have lost all their attractiveness as such, and in a short time the only trace of them and their gardens will be possibly the place name which may in some way or other be retained.

Smedley Lane was even then a popular residential thoroughfare, the occupants of the houses including some very successful business men. The residents in the lane in 1824 included John Boardman, gentleman; John Chippendall, the calico printer to whom I have previously referred, and who lived at Beech Hill (still standing); the Rev. C. W. Ethelston, who resided at Smedley Hill and who was one of the magistrates present at Peterloo; E. Howarth, calico printer, who lived at Smedley Bank, and Thomas Taylor, fustian manufacturer, whose warehouse was at 6 M'Donald's Lane. Smedley Hall was occupied by Mr. R. Potter, a retired brewer, and on the banks of the river were the calendering works of George Ashton and Drinkwater's bleachworks. The village constable's name, C. Bates appears in the list, as also do the names of the keepers of two toll bars. William Jagger kept the White Smithy bar and George Thornton kept the bar that formerly stood at the end of Smedley Lane. In Chapel Lane was the commercial school of John Lea; the only other resident's name included in the list being that of Peter Seale, gentleman. Tetlow Fold was the address of W. Garnett, merchant, of St. James' Square, whose brother, Robert, lived at Oak Hill, a fine house that stood near the end of Tetlow Lane, on a site now covered by rows of small houses. George Grundy and Benjamin Potter also lived in the fold. The banker, E. Loyd, resided at Green Hill, and Mrs. Henshaw at Stonewall. Both these houses have been previously dealt with. Broomfield, the former home of James Halliwell, appears to have been divided into two residences in one of which Robert Christie, drysalter of Brown Street lived, and in the other Samuel Edge, attorney, lived.

IN 1838.

By 1838 York Street, now the lower portion of Cheetham Hill Road, was being gradually built up as has been noted in a previous chapter. The houses on the right hand side of the street, going in the direction of Cheetham Hill, were built close up to the road, but those on the opposite side had short gardens in front of them. Quite early on in the history of the thoroughfare the buildings on the right hand side were used as shops, but most, if not all, that were built on the opposite side were used as private houses. In all there were fifty-four tenements occupied from New Bridge Street to Stocks House. As the directories of those days are wanting in the clearness of description that characterises those of to-day, in the case under notice no house numbers or names are given save in two cases where successive numberings as of adjacent terraces, the numbers 1 to 9 being duplicated. A few of the names in the list are worthy of note. In the first place we find that of John Redfern, who had brick-making works at Cheetwood. Seventy years ago the industry must have been in its infancy so far as the Cheetham Hill Road district is concerned; to-day it is reducing to a state of desolation all the available land in the district. Bit by bit the old village of Cheetwood is being pulled down and the sites of the houses and gardens added to the already extensive brick crofts. Amongst the residents was the Rev. Nicholas Germon, who was second master of the Grammar School, and rector of St. Peter's Church. A clerical neighbour of his was the Rev. Robert Cox Clifton, who was elected a Fellow of the Collegiate Church in 1843, and who was in 1838 clerk at the same church. He was the author of a number of pamphlets on educational and other questions; and died at

Somerton in 1861. Next door neighbour to Mr. Clifton was Mr. E. Dodgshon, cotton spinner, who was one of the first councillors returned to represent the New Cross Ward in the city council. Another resident was Thomas Wroe, who was Comptroller under the Manchester Police Commissioners, and was one of the first managers of the gas works; and near to him resided John Fothergill, one of the best known engravers of the day, whose printing office was in Prince's Court, Market Street. His name is to be seen on many of the fine specimens of the engraver's art to be found attached to tradesmen's announcements of seventy years ago.

Beyond Stocks House, save at Temple, there were no houses on the right hand side until Smedley Lane was reached. the first houses being those of John Chippendall and Edward Loyd previously referred to. A resident of Cheetham Hill at this time was George Condy, barrister, who became Editor and joint proprietor of the *Manchester and Salford Advertiser*, and a Commissioner in Bankruptcy. He was a man of great accomplishments, and had few equals as a critic of music, painting, and the drama. His son in later years was the manufacturer of the well-known disinfectant, Condy's Fluid. Many of the residents of that time have already been mentioned. One place name of that date is curious. It was Cheetham Recess, and in it were situated eight houses. In Tetlow Fold were a number of fine residences, and in Halliwell Lane about half a dozen merchants resided together with the families of not more than ten other burgesses. Several of the mansions still survive, but in consequence of the large amount of building that has taken place during the last thirty years their situation is very different from what it was. The making of Waterloo Road, for some time regarded as a blunder by many persons, the opening out of Queen's Road, and the formation of the district known generally as Hightown with its scores of streets and thousands of houses, have completely changed the appearance of this side of the city.

A word or two may be said with reference to the creation of Hightown. The story of its origin and development was told in the *City News* a few years ago. It arose in a curious fashion. A well-to-do woollen merchant carried on business in King Street in 1845. His name was Daniel Percival and he had previously been partner in a smaller business in St. Mary's Gate, but had paid out his partner and had then removed to larger premises at 24 King Street. One of his assistants helped himself to the cash that passed through his hands to such an extent that although Mr. Percival's business increased neither the bank balance nor the stock increased. Ultimately the defalcations were detected, the offender was sentenced to fourteen years transportation, and some £4500 was recovered by Mr. Percival. After due consideration he decided to use his windfall in building houses in the suburbs of the town, and being joined in the venture by two business friends, Messrs. Bishop and Hewitt, of Leeds, the tract of land lying between Cheetwood and Cheetham Hill was purchased. The name Hightown was given to the district in compliment to his two friends by Mr. Percival, it being the name of a suburb of Leeds. Building operations were commenced, but by 1857 only a small number of streets had been formed, and the district retained much of its original rural charm. The writer of the article previously referred to, speaking on this point says: "At the further end of Walnut street, an agreeable plantation flourished bordering a fine stretch of meadow land, which sloped away down into a pretty valley. In this valley nestled Blue Bell Clough, a pretty romantic dingle watered by a clear brook. In the spring the valley was rich with the bloom of the hawthorn, the fragrance of which mingled with of great numbers of wild flowers. There was a public path through the meadows, and on summer evenings a ramble to and along the valley was a constant delight to those living near. On the further side of the valley—we can scarcely realise it now—stood Gilt's farm, an old fashioned rustic looking place, the cattle from which gazed picturesquely on the slopes what time the mavis and the blackbird piped in the dell below."

Soon after the time referred to Marlborough Road was made, and then came a more rapid change in the appearance of the district. Fields once covered with corn were now covered with houses. New streets were made, the old thoroughfares lost their rural appearance; Tetlow Fold, Tetlow Lane, and Halliwell Lane ceased to be desirable places of residence for the wealthy, and in the course of a generation the appearance of the districts had been completely tranformed. That useful but objectionable aid to the speculative builder, the public tip, made its appearance; and before some people had time to realise the fact, Blue Bell Valley, with its early summer delights, had disappeared for ever, buried underneath a vile tip, on the top of which was built rows of houses, some of such a wretched condition that they fell down before they were finished. Within the last twenty years the rate of building has been more rapid than previously, and although some of the present houses are fairly well situated, the bulk of the population is housed in houses crowded as closely together as the building by-laws will permit, and as innocent of a garden or the appearance of suburban conditions of life as obtains in Ancoats or Hulme. It will be marvellous if another thirty years does not see the development of another slum problem.

Elizabeth Street and the adjacent streets mark the site of the fields that bounded both sides of Dirty Lane. The making of Cheetham Park with its flower beds and bowling green appreciated as it is to-day, will be even more valuable to future generations, as it is probable that another twenty years will see the removal of the few remaining patches of green to be seen to-day.

The erection of the tram shed in Queen's Road marked the latest development in the system of public conveyance, the earliest form of which was the occasional omnibus run by a man named Penketh more than seventy years ago. Penketh afterwards sold it to John Ramsbottom, and continued to drive for him. Ramsbottom was a coach proprietor who resided at Temple Cottage. He increased the number of vehicles, and later they were sold to Greenwood, Clough and Turner, who ran them until the partnership was dissolved, when Robert Turner retained the Cheetham Hill business, Greenwood resuming possession of the Pendleton branch. From these beginnings has developed our fine electric tramway system, with its millions of passengers annually and small army of workers.

HEATON PARK AND HEATON HALL.

Manchester's most important park became the property of the ratepayers on March 14th, 1902. Six years earlier the Park had been offered to the Manchester Corporation for the sum of £250,000. The matter was referred to a committee of the City Council, but after investigation that body were of opinion that the price asked was excessive, and that, therefore, they could not recommend the purchase. This was the cause of much disappointment to many, especially in view of the fact that the chance of securing Trafford Park had passed. There was consequently an undercurrent of opinion favourable to the purchase of the park, which opinion became gradually stronger until when in 1901 the matter was once again brought forward, it was merely a question of terms. Negotiations were re-opened, and a deputation was sent to London to make a definite offer of £190,000 for the 650 acres of land which comprised the park. This proposal was rejected, but was succeeded by another one which should include some 38 acres of land that lay between the Middleton Road side of the park and the City boundary. By this means it was hoped to include the park within the city boundary at some future time. For this land, together with the park, £230,000 was offered, and, after a small plot of land near to the Grand Lodge had been included in the contract, the bargain was settled, and the former home of the Earls of Wilton became the property of the citizens of Manchester.

The park is situated to the north of the city, the Grand Lodge—which forms the principal entrance—being about three and a half miles from St. Ann's Square on the Bury Old Road.

THE FORMER OWNERS OF THE PARK.

The Manchester Corporation purchased the park from Arthur George Egerton, fifth Earl of Wilton. It formed only a portion of the estate of the Earl of Wilton, whose family at one time owned the whole of the land comprised within the parish of Prestwich, with the exception of one cottage at Catty Green.

I shall endeavour to sketch in a few words the succession of ownership to the park. It formerly belonged to the estate of the Langleys, who lived at Agecroft Hall; but about five hundred and fifty years ago it passed by the marriage of Margaret, the daughter and co-heiress of Sir Robert Langley, to Richard Holland of Denton. The Hollands are one of our oldest families, and are descended from Sir Stephen Holland, of Skevington, in the County of Lincoln, who was a leading character in the reign of Edward the Confessor. The Hollands of Heaton and Denton formed one branch of the family, and the name frequently appears in the historical records of the county. In 1582, Richard Holland, of Heaton House, took active steps in the interests of the king; but in later years the male line died out, and the Heaton estate passed by the marriage of Elizabeth, sister and co-heiress of Edward Holland, to Sir John Egerton, of Wrinehill and Farthington. This was another branch of the family which is represented to-day by the Egertons of Tatton and those of Worsley. Sir John was succeeded in his inheritance by his eldest son, Sir Holland, who in turn was succeeded by his fifth son, Sir Thomas Grey Egerton. Later again, Sir Rowland Egerton married the only sister and heiress of Thomas, Lord Grey de Wilton, and from them was descended Sir Thomas Egerton, of Egerton, and Oulton, who was created Earl of Wilton in 1784. He married Eleanor, the youngest daughter and co-heiress of Sir Ralph Assheton, Bart., and was succeeded by his son Thomas. The last named married Mary Margaret Stanley, daughter of Edward, the eleventh Earl of Derby. This lady's mother was of humble parentage, but in early life, showing great histrionic talents, she became a popular actress. Miss Farren was one of the first actresses to appear on the stage of Manchester's first Theatre Royal, which was built at the corner of Spring Gardens and York Street in 1775. She did not remain long on the stage, but married the Earl of Derby. Their younger daughter became the second Countess of Wilton. It was during the time of the second Earl that many alterations were made in the mansion and grounds. He also organised a series of race meetings, of which some account will be given on a later page, together with some interesting reminiscences of the home life of the family about the same time. The second Earl was a man of varied accomplishments, publishing a volume entitled *Sports and Pursuits of the English People*, and having studied surgery, was enabled to render first aid to Mr. Huskisson, the Liverpool M.P., when that gentleman met with his fatal accident on the occasion of the opening of the Liverpool and Manchester Railway.

THE HALL.

Heaton House as a building is not of interest either to the architect or the historian. It was built from designs of James Wyatt, and it is stated that "without identifying itself with any of the five orders, approaches nearest to the Ionic." Internally there are several interesting features, including a fine staircase, and the decorations in certain of the larger rooms. Further reference will be made to the paintings in the billiard room; but beyond the few features mentioned there is little worthy of note to be seen in the mansion. The library walls were formerly hidden by a series of magnificent mahogany book-cases, which have been removed; the music room holds an organ, now of little value owing to long disuse and exposure to damp; and in the circular room are to be seen some charming specimens of ceiling decoration. The organ was built by a well-known builder, Green, who also erected an organ for the Gentlemen's Concert Hall in Fountain Street. As will be gathered from further pages, the mansion has in its day been visited by many notable characters, and when arrangements are made for the use of some of the more important rooms for the purpose of an art gallery or exhibition, the citizens have opportunities for inspecting the few points of interest there are in the hall.

THE PICTURES.

The pictures in what was formerly the billiard room

Heaton Hall.

have aroused much interest amongst visitors. The name of the artist and the subjects they depict are matters concerning which no definite information is forthcoming. It has been stated that they were the work of Angellica Kauffmann, a painter.born at Cairo in 1741, who spent fifteen years of her life—from 1766 to 1781—in England, where, in addition to other work, she did much decoration of this description in connection with a number of residences in London and the provinces. Other persons are of opinion that the pictures were the work of certain fairly competent Italian painters who were brought from London for the purpose of decorating certain parts of the hall. The subjects of the pictures are also left to conjecture. They, however, contain within themselves clues which enable the visitor versed in classical lore to name the subjects of some of them. It is believed that the whole of the series represent incidents recorded in ancient mythology. To give merely a list of the subjects would convey little information, and to attempt to give an explanation of each would be beyond our present limits. The stories represented by two of the pictures may be given as typical of the whole. Thus we have the representation of Romulus and Remus, who were the sons of Silvia and the god Mars. As infants they were exposed in a cradle, and a flood suddenly arising they were carried in the cradle to the foot of the Palatine. There they were suckled by a wolf until one, Faustulus, the king's shepherd, saw them, took them home to his wife and brought them up. When grown to manhood they slew Amulius, who had caused them to be exposed. Another of the pictures represents Arion, who was a famous musician, and was supposed to be the inventor of dithyrambic poetry. He was afraid of being murdered for his wealth, and consequently threw himself into the sea. There he found refuge on the back of a dolphin, whom he charmed with his music, and by whom he was conveyed to a place of safety. Then we have the representation of Narcissus, who, according to the Grecian fable, fell in love with his own reflection in a fountain, and, having pined away because he could not kiss it, was changed into the flower that bears his name. The other pictures represent subjects belonging to the same class, and were probably the stock pictures of some of the Italian artists of the latter part of the nineteenth century.

THE PARK.

The park occupies nearly 650 acres of land, of which 600 acres are open fields. The whole, together with 42 acres of land, were purchased by the Manchester Corporation in March, 1902, for the sum of £230,000. The park wall is four miles long, is ten feet high, and is eighteen inches thick at the bottom. There are six lodges, with gates, by which visitors can enter the park. The principal one is known as the Grand Lodge, standing near the corner of Bury Old Road and Sheepfoot Lane. The Station Lodge is opposite to the Lancashire and Yorkshire Railway Station at Heaton Park Village, and St. Margaret's Lodge is near to the church of that name in Hodge Lane. These three entrances are all in close proximity to the tramway route along Bury Old Road. The North Lodge stands on the Dridle Road, and the other two entrances are on the Middleton Road, which is also a tramways route. At the entrance formerly known as the Heaton Gate Lodge the Manchester tramcars enter the park.

The hall, known as Heaton House, has already been described. From the elevated ground on which it stands many extensive views can be obtained. Close by is a round building known as the Temple, which appears to have served the purpose of an observatory. Lying between the Temple and Old Hall Lane are two sheets of water, and a little distance away is a third one. All three would furnish good sport to the angler, as in the second Earl's time they were well stocked with fish. Their retired situation attracts numbers of wild duck, many of which birds may often be seen there. Adjacent to the hall are the gardens and pleasure grounds, which furnish a number of delightful walks. There is little in the way of systematic ornamental gardening attempted in the park, but in summer time the flower beds adjoining the greenhouses, and those near the conservatory next to the hall, are gay with colour. A bandstand has been erected on the lower ground near to the junction of the roads from Middleton Road and the Grand Lodge, and shelters have been provided in various parts of the park.

The greater proportion of the park is covered by open field land, over which visitors may roam at will. Dotted over the park are a number of small plantations, which serve as breeding grounds for innumerable wild birds, who appear to appreciate the immunity from danger that they enjoy within its borders. There may be found in addition to the throstle, the skylark, and the blackbird, several varieties of linnet, the yellow-hammer, the chaffinch, the willow wren, and several members of the wren family. The lapwing is not so common as in some districts round Manchester, and partridges and pheasants appear to have permanently vacated an area where formerly they abounded. The birds which, however, demand most attention from visitors are the peacocks, whose display of gorgeously coloured feathers are a source of never-ending delight to the juveniles. The latter have also enjoyed the sight of the rabbits feeding on the lawns. About four years ago the greater number of these animals were destroyed, ferrets and nets being the means of destruction adopted. The process, however, stopped short of extermination, and it is satisfactory to know to know that once again this delightful feature of country life is to be seen in our park. The introduction of the deer was a commendable experiment, and it only remains for the Committee to supply better winter quarters in order to make the lot of these timid animals as comfortable as it should be.

HOME LIFE AT HEATON PARK IN 1830.

Fanny Kemble, the well-known actress of fifty years ago, furnishes some very interesting particulars of the home life at Heaton as she saw it more than 70 years ago. In several of her letters she makes several references which will be of interest to present-day visitors to the park. The first of these is contained in a letter dated September 3rd, 1830, in which she says: "We have gone out to Heaton every morning after rehearsal, and come with the Wiltons in the evening to act.

I think to-night we shall sleep there after the play and come up with the W's after dinner to-morrow. They have expected us to spend some days with them, and perhaps after our Birmingham engagement we might be able to do so. Heaton is a charming specimen of a fine country house, and Lady W. a charming specimen of a fine lady; she is handsome, stately, and gentle. I like Lord W.: he is clever, or rather, accomplished and refined." Writing four days later from Birmingham, Miss Kemble gives us a peep at an old-time celebration very popular in our grandfather's days, but now merely a memory of the past. After referring to other matters she goes on to say that "I must tell you a curious little bit of ancientry which I saw at Heaton which greatly delighted me—a rush bearing." She then describes the waggon piled up with rushes arranged in the form of a stack, with two men sitting at the top holding nosegays. This was drawn by a team of the Earl of Wilton's finest farm horses, covered with scarlet cloths and decked with ribbons, bells and flowers. Following the cart there went "twelve country lads and lasses dancing the real old Morris dance." "A very good village band" provided the music, and under a "flowery canopy walked a man and woman covered with finery and representing Adam and Eve." The rear of the procession was brought up by a "fool fantastically dressed." The whole party drew up in front of the hall and danced for the entertainment of the visitors. Miss Kemble paid the promised visit to Heaton Park, and on September 18th we find her writing: "I am at this moment writing in a drawing room filled with people at Heaton

(Lord W.'s place), taking up my pen to write to you, and laying it down to speak with others." She had travelled to Manchester from Liverpool as a passenger on one of the trains that formed the procession by which the railway had been opened. After recording the incidents of the journey, notable amongst which was the fatal accident to Mr. Huskisson, she speaks of accompanying Lady W. to Heaton Park. On the Sunday preceding, the Duke of Wellington, who opened the railway, was a guest at the hall, on which occasion a large house party was entertained. Miss Kemble further speaks of Lord Wilton reading evening prayers to the servants and visitors, and refers to his being a good organist and that he "delighted in that noble instrument, a fine specimen of which adorns one of the drawing rooms of Heaton." She tells us that her father said that Lady Wilton bore a strong resemblance to her mother, the celebrated Miss Farren. The names of some of the distinguished visitors she met at Heaton are given; and, after referring to the "elegant magnificence of the mode of life at Heaton," she says of the park: "Heaton is looking lovely in all the beauty of its autumnal foliage lighted by bright and autumnal skies."

HEATON PARK RACES.

No account of Heaton Park, however brief, would be complete without some reference to the race meetings that were formerly held there. The first of these gatherings took place on Tuesday, September 25th, 1827, on which occasion the park was thrown open to the public, who took full advantage of the privilege granted to them. Many aristocrats also attended; the Duke of Beaufort driving a dashing four in hand. The finest turnout was that of Mr. John Knowles, the stage-coach proprietor, who ran the Peveril of the Peak coach to London, and whose son was in later years the popular manager of the Theatre Royal. Mr. Knowles' turnout on this occasion consisted of six beautiful piebalds. The crowds in the park were so great that the Earl ordered the gates to be closed at three o'clock, to the disappointment of many who arrived later in the afternoon. The result was that in 1828 it was announced that pedestrians would not be admitted to the meeting. Consequently all varieties of queer looking vehicles were called into requisition. At first the meetings only extended over two days, but in 1829 they were extended to three days. The sport was not of a high class description, but was frequently very interesting to Manchester people.

Perhaps the most popular owner who ran horses at Heaton Park was Mr. Thomas Houldsworth, who lived at Portland Place, Piccadilly, in a house which forms a portion of the present Queen's Hotel, and whose mill in Newton Street has made way for the new Post Office building. His nephew, Sir William Houldsworth, is well-known to the Manchester people of to-day. Thomas Houldsworth's colours were popular; and there was great excitement in 1831 when his horse, Vanish, defeated Mr. Sadler's Jocko, who a year before had won two gold cups. The race was for a gold cup given by townspeople and known as the Manchester Cup. The same race in 1832 produced much fine sport, Perseverance winning, with Vanish only half a neck behind. One of the guests of Lord Wilton in that year was Tom Thumb, who was driven through the park by his lordship.

In 1834 an exciting race was run for Mr. King's Gold Cup, the winner only leading by a few inches. In 1835 a change was introduced, and for the first time professional jockies were allowed to compete in the various races with gentlemen riders. At the same time the system of exclusiveness was abandoned, and tickets of admission to the park were given to all respectable persons applying for them. In that year a curious incident occured in the race for the Heaton Park Stakes, when Mr. E. Peel's Tarick fell about three-quarters of a mile from home, but, getting up, continued the race, and finally came in first, but without rider. In 1836 a former Derby winner, Mr. Bowe's Mundig, ran for the Manchester Cup, along with nine others, but was beaten by Mr. Dawson's Locomotive. Lord Robert Grosvenor acted as steward of the races, and he, together with a number of gentry, patronised a performance of the "Merchant of Venice" at the Theatre Royal, Fountain Street, for which performance Mr. Charles Kean, Mr. Browne, and Mr. and Mrs. Tayleure came from London for one night only. This was Charles Kean's last appearance on the Manchester stage, and at the close of the performance he delivered an address in which he made reference to his debut on our boards thirty-four years before. In 1837 the curious feature was presented of two horses reversing their positions in two races in the course of three days. In the Heaton Park Stakes race Lord Chesterfield's Scroggins won a remarkably easy victory over Lord Suffield's Cowboy; but in the race for the Silver Vase, two days later, Cowboy won by a length and a half in a better run contest. The great contest at these meetings was for the Manchester Cup, which in 1838 was worth two hundred sovereigns. On that occasion the winner was the Earl of Wilton's Jagger. This was the last of the Heaton Park meetings, and in 1839 the races were removed to Liverpool.

WITHY GROVE.

PART I.

As we pass along the busy crowded streets of the great city of to-day the mind dwells upon that which meets the eye; and most people are disinclined to attempt to conjure up a representation of what the town or village looked like centuries ago. When, on the other hand, we find ourselves in its streets on a quiet Sunday morning, when passers-by are few, and when we have a leisure hour to spare, we find it easy to carry our imagination back into the dim past. To the intelligent observer, in spite of modern changes, there are not wanting objects that catch the eye, and make the retrospective glance a matter of intense interest. For example, turning out of the modern street with a modern name, Corporation Street, into Withy Grove, the thinking man is at once carried back into the Manchester of Queen Elizabeth's time, when Withingreave, as it was then called, was a pleasant country lane. Well tilled fields bounded it on either side, and in 1569 we are told that Roger Bexwicke became the tenant of a portion of those fields, paying as rent for the fields and a barn the sum of eight shillings per annum to the lord of the manor. At the corner of Hanging Ditch and Withingreave there stood a few cottages; a little distance up the lane

The Seven Stars Inn.

was a picturesque black and white inn, still standing and known as the Seven Stars; and at the top of the lane, where it turned to the left and took the name of Shudehill, stood Withingreave Hall, to which most of the farm land hereabouts belonged. Hedgerows bounded the lane, and down one side ran a stream, fed by the waters coming from the higher land. In this respect Withingreave was very much like many a pleasant lane to be found in Cheshire. The stream followed its course down Hanging Ditch and under the Hanging Bridge, falling into the river near to the old Salford Bridge. In its course down our lane it probably widened out somewhat, and on its marshy banks there probably grew numbers of willows or withies as they were called. In the days when the black and white type of a house was built withies were in considerable demand, because by weaving them into a network between the timbers that formed the framework of the buildings they served as a foundation on which was spread the tempered clay or daub, of which the buildings were so largely constructed. In this it is believed that the modern name of Withy Grove originated. It takes us back to very early days; and seeing that there has survived one building of that period we cannot do better at this stage than visit the ancient hostel known as the Seven Stars Inn.

THE SEVEN STARS INN.

Before we examine into its history let us, however, dispose of an error, often repeated, in connection with it. We are told: "According to the County Records preserved in the Record Office, Lancaster Castle (since removed to London), the Seven Stars in Withy Grove has been a licensed hostelry for a period of 511 years, the first license having been granted in the reign of Edward III. A.D. 1356." This was written in 1867. According to the statement the Seven Stars has been a licensed house for more than five and a half centuries. Now for historic fact. The first mention that we have of a license in connection with a public house is dated 1551, and before that date anyone could sell ale. In Manchester in the first half of the sixteenth century any burgess could sell ale providing that he could provide two beds, and also that he exhibited the sign of a hand outside his house if he had a barrel on tap. It was not until 1579 that the Steward took action with reference to non-licensed houses, and he issued an order that any person keeping such a house and selling ale therein should be fined ten shillings. The Seven Stars has probably been a licensed house for three and a half centuries. This is not the only incorrect statement made with reference to the old building. We are told that in the cellars is an exceedingly old arch which is the entrance to a secret passage affording communication with the Collegiate Church (Cathedral) and Ordsall Hall. This is all a myth. No such passage exists. Then again we are told that Guy Fawkes visited Manchester, and was concealed at the old inn; and to-day we have "Ye Guy Faux Chamber" pointed out to us as the room wherein he stayed. Again we say, not correct. Harrison Ainsworth makes out a very plausible tale, but in this, as in many other cases his statements do not tally with historic records.

Another legend has to do with some blackened metal

vessels to be seen in a cupboard in the bar. We are told that during the Civil War a regiment of dragoons under Sir Thomas Fairfax, marching to the relief of Nantwich in 1644, were quartered at the Seven Stars, and that whilst here they buried their mess plate. During some structural alterations a few years ago a quantity of silver plate was found, and was carefully placed in the glass case referred to. This, we are told, was the mess plate of the Puritan dragoons. When visiting the inn on several occasions I have asked for permission to examine the reputed plate, but have been told that they are locked up and that the key is lost. A gentleman who examined them says of them: "The articles were blackened no doubt, but not with age, nor were they of silver or engraved for any regiment. Upon turning them up I found, as I expected, upon the bottoms of them the name of Dixon and Son, of Sheffield. They were of their manufacture and were made of their Britannia metal only."

Coming down another century we find that when Charles Stuart visited Manchester in 1745 some of his soldiers slept at the hostel where Colonel Townley enrolled a Manchester regiment. One of the references in the Court Leet Records to the inn bears the date December 11th, 1745, and is to the effect that John Hulme of the Seven Stars was paid 5s. 6d. for horses and expresses, possibly in connection with the visit of the young pretender. In the early part of the last century the inn was the resort of a number of literary men, including James Weatherley and Elijah Ridings and of many wits of the town, while Gregson wrote later of it as follows :—

> "But country folks most chiefly go to fill
> James Hudson's long room, Seven Stars, Shudehill,
> Where, as if for wagers, they their meals devour,
> And only allow themselves one poor half-hour.
> Scarce wait for grace ; 'God bless it' some will say ;
> Others cry 'to it'; have not time to pray.
> The dinner ended, appetite allayed,
> What's always uppermost, they think, but trade ;
> Quickly return to business, 'all alive'
> To get it done, and clear away by five."

But although the historic data attached to the Seven Stars is meagre, the place is most interesting and well worth a visit. The old house with its quaint gables, its black and white front, and its primitive sliding windows, will convince the most sceptical of its antiquity ; while the low rooms with their black beams and oak panelling, all black with age, will repay inspection. There was formerly a collection of fine old oak furniture in many of the rooms, but this was dispersed by auction recently. One object remains to which special attention may be called. On a post at the bottom of the stairs is nailed a horse shoe to which a pathetic interest attaches. In the days of the Press Gang, a century ago, a farm servant was passing up Withy Grove leading a horse that had cast a shoe, which he carried in his hand. As he passed the inn the Gang, who were billetted there, rushed out and pressed the unfortunate man into the king's service. No excuse being available, he handed over the horse to the care of a friend who undertook to take it to its owner. The pressed man asked the landlord to allow him to nail the horse shoe to the post, saying that he would call for it on his return from the wars. The horse shoe was never claimed, but is still to be seen, awaiting in vain the return of the claimant—a silent reminder of the terrible days that England passed through a century ago. With this we leave the old inn with the expression of the hope that whatever changes may be deemed necessary in the city, the old Seven Stars may be spared to remind future generations of the England and Manchester of the past.

Hyde's Cross is surrounded by much mystery. Aston says that there was formerly a cross there and that cattle being sold there it came to be known as Hyde's (Hides) Cross. It has been suggested that the cross was formerly regarded as a sanctuary for certain classes of offenders, but there was a sanctuary house in Smithy Door; and there is no reliable evidence to hand showing that the Withy Grove site was ever devoted to such a purpose.

WITHY GROVE.

PART II.

AS IT WAS IN 1745 and 1793.

When Casson and Berry issued their plans, Withing Grove was semi-rural in appearance, although houses appear to have extended along its entire length on both sides. Behind most of the houses there were gardens, and beyond the gardens open fields covered a large portion of the area between there and Market Street Lane. On the opposite side of Withy Grove Garden Lane gave access to open fields, although Merchant Street and Union Street had been formed and were pretty well built up. The plans give us very little in the way of details concerning our thoroughfare beyond the bare facts just stated. We, therefore, turn to Laurent's plan issued nearly sixty years later, and find much more to interest us.

The whole of the street had been built up, although some open ground remained in the neighbourhood of Watling Street. The lower length of the street, from the corner of Hanging Ditch to the corner of Garden Street, was designated Hyde's Cross, Withy Grove extending from Garden Street to Nicholas Croft, where Shudehill commenced. The Boar's Head Inn stood at the corner of Toad Lane, and Cock Gates gave access to the land behind the inn. Coldhouse, interesting on account of its chapel, Garden Street, the site of Manchester's first Infirmary, and Bradshaw Street, so named after Bradshaw Hall, the town house of the Bradshaw family, appear on our plan ; and the space now occupied by the Hen Market is marked off from the street by posts.

Several of the buildings of a century ago have survived. The Seven Stars has already been mentioned, but something remains to be said concerning the Old Boars' Head, Bradshaw Hall, and Withingreave Hall.

TWO OLD-TIME FORMS OF SPORT.

Although the Old Boar's Head is one of the oldest licensed houses in the city, it has little about it of historic note. We cannot trace out the connection of any leading character with it, nor is its name associated with any great event or movement, beyond the fact that in the earlier decades of the last century occasional stage coaches made it a starting point. It was, however, connected with two forms of sport, popular with our forefathers of a century and a half ago, of which mementos have been handed down to us.

One of these sports was bear-baiting, a form of sport not usually associated with our city. The source of our information is a rough but interesting sketch depicting the indulgence in the sport by a number of townsfolk. The drawing is contained in a scrapbook in the possession of a local public body, and seeing that it depicts a form of the sport not usually known it may be described somewhat fully. The encounter is represented as taking place in the open roadway in front of the Old Boar's Head, and the date is said to have been 1749. The spectator is standing near to the corner of Hanging Ditch and Hyde's Cross. In the near background is the inn with its projecting swinging sign, and in the further distance are some of the houses in Toad Lane, since removed to make Corporation Street. In the centre of the roadway, at the crossing, the bear is tethered by the nose to a stake driven into the ground. So short is the rope by which he is secured that it is doubtful whether he could do more than stand erect. Every time that he attempted to move forward his head would be brought nearer to the ground. He would therefore be considerably less dangerous to his tormentors. The baiting was done by wheelbarrows, and bladders attached to long sticks. Around the bear, and forming a ring are a number of interested spectators. In the sketch a man is represented as striking the bear in the side with the wheel of a barrow, whilst others similarly armed are waiting an opportunity of getting in a stroke. This was evidently done to draw off the attention of the bear from a man who had just hit him over the head with a bladder. The onlookers seemed to get a large amount of pleasure and excitement from the sport. I have made many inquiries, but have failed to elicit any information as to the indulgence in this particular form of bear-baiting in any other part of the country. It says much for the state of trade in the town in 1749 when such a spectacle was possible in the middle of a principal street.

The second reference is to a note written by Thomas Barritt in one of his manuscript common-place books. It refers to 1750 and thereabouts, and is as follows:

" When I was a boy about eight years old, a noted prize fighter came to Manchester, by name Thomas Barret, an old man with his face cut and scarred all over, so that for the most part he went by the name of 'Old Chopping-block.' He taught the science of defence (or what I should think was sometimes offence) in a large room at the Old Boar's Head, Hyde's Cross. While in town he articled with a stranger to show their feats of arms in public, in a yard near Salford Chapel; at which place I attended to see the exhibition, which was performed upon a stage in the manner following: First, the champions entered the lists in their shirts, and bareheaded, each with a quarter staff about two yards long, and as thick as the handle of a pikel. These they brandished and whirled about with surprising dexterity; not forgetting every now and then to reach each other a lusty souse upon the sides, shoulders, or head, which was in no ways displeasing to the spectators. This exercise being ended, and a little time spent in refreshing, the combatants approached each other with basket-hilted broadswords, and each a target (a large shield or buckler) upon their left arm; seconds likewise being appointed and upon the stage with poles, to prevent them going to extremities. In a little while both targets, not being covered with leather, were slit in pieces, and 'Old Chopping-block' after this received a cut upon the cheek, near the nose. He immediately returned the compliment, cutting his antagonist directly upon the brow; by which their faces were almost covered with blood. After some few flourishes with their weapons, old Barret received another wound on his face, near the former, which he did not seem to approve; and, spying an opening in his adversary, gave him such a slice on the forehead, and with such earnestness, that the seconds, thinking it not prudent that the business should be continued any longer, parted them. This affair, however, not subsiding, a second challenge was given and place appointed, which was the Old Boar's Head yard, where I again attended a few days later. The fellows again mounted the stage with swords; but old Barret taking the advantage, cut his antagonist in the side, which was declared unfair play. Thus this combat ended, and was the last sword-play I ever heard of in England."

These two reminiscences give us interesting glimpses of the forms of recreation that were popular in the Manchester of a century and a half ago. With them we leave the Old Boar's Head and in the course of the next few chapters I purpose passing up one side of the old thoroughfare and down the other, noting the chief points of interest as we pass.

WITHY GROVE.

PART III.

SOME OLD STREET NAMES.

Like the name Withy Grove, the names of some of the minor streets running out of it take us back to the earlier days of the city. The name of Cock Gates has never been satisfactorily explained. Had the cock-pit not been located nearer to Market Street one would have been inclined to associate it with the one-time popular sport, but under the circumstances no such suggestion is admissable. There is some difficulty also with reference to another old place name that disappeared when the premises occupied by *Sporting Chronicle* newspaper offices were erected nearly thirty years ago. Huntsman's Court seems to take us back to the days when the jovial huntsmen, after following the chase over the Coldhouse and other meadows, would assemble at the hospitable board of the squire of Withingreave Hall. As a matter of coincidence or otherwise, the names of several of the older inns in the neighbourhood seem to remind us of those times. Not to mention the Old Boar's Head, we have the Hare and Hounds, the Roebuck, and the Dog and Partridge, and not far away was the Spread Eagle.

THE FIRST INFIRMARY.

Garden Street, originally Garden Lane, took its name from a fine garden which was formerly attached to a house standing in Withy Grove. The street is principally notable because it was the site of Manchester's first infirmary. In these days, when Manchester's magnificent new Infirmary is demanding so much attention, it will be well to recount the story of its origin as told by Aston. He says: "The infirmary owes its origin to several worthy and public spirited characters, in the year 1752. But, notwithstanding, many were anxious for the establishment of a charity, which was to restore health to the sick, and soundness to the lame, many difficulties seem to have arisen, which retarded the ultimate establishment. Several meetings were held, but nothing was resolved upon, till a gentleman, whose name deserves to be held in everlasting and honourable remembrance, whose benevolence was active, and whose judgment and knowledge of the human heart, and its best propensities, led him to conclude that an infirmary only wanted a beginning, and that maturity of means would be the necessary consequence, from the prevalent disposition of the superior class of the inhabitants of Manchester. From this conclusion the late Joseph Bancroft, Esq. acted; and with a noble spirit he offered (if anyone else would join him in the plan) to defray all the expenses of an infirmary for one year; provided the present respectable and venerable surgeon, Charles White, Esq. would give his assistance in his professional capacity." The result was the renting and furnishing of a house in Garden Street, Withy Grove, which was opened for the relief of out-patients on June 24th, 1752. A month later the first in-patients were admitted, and in the course of the first year seventy-five in-patients and 249 out-patients. During the year donations and legacies to the value of £361 12s. 0d. were received, and the subscription list amounted to £488 0s. 6d. In 1753 it was decided to erect a building that should accommodate forty patients, and two years later the building on Piccadilly was opened.

We have now reached the limit of Withy Grove, and crossing over encounter the end of Sugar Lane, now the recognised centre for the carriers who travel between the country districts and the city. The name is a curious one, and from time to time attempts have been made to trace its origin. Hitherto the efforts have been unsuccessful, and to-day all we know about it is that it existed three centuries ago, but is not mentioned or in any way denoted on Casson and Berry's map of nearly a century and a half later. The isolated reference to the thoroughfare takes us back to the terrible plague days, when the dreaded affliction made serious inroads on the population of our towns. In 1605 the pestilence raged fearfully in Manchester, and from the Collegiate Church registers we find that one of the victims is thus described: "1605, Maye 25—Richard Boile, in ye Sugar Lane, Buried." The next reference to our street is to be found in the Court Leet Records for 1738, when John Holme was fined for failing to abate a nuisance at the bottom of Sugar Lane. In the closing decade of the century the street was an active centre for recruiting for the "Marines." In a broadside that has survived, a stirring appeal was made to all "spirited heroes" who wished "to enlist in this valuable corps" to apply to Serjeant Aylward at the sign of the Mason's Arms, Sugar Lane, where they would be handsomely entertained.

In 1838 Sugar Lane had as a tenant within its boundary, Nicholson Varley, who is described as a chymist. Mr. Varley was a relation of James Varley, one time drysalter and inventor of a process for making chloride of lime, and afterwards a hosier in Oldham Street and Market Street, and whose daughter as Mrs. Banks gave us the most interesting of the various novels that have been written with a local foundation. Mr. Varley's neighbours in Sugar Lane were a very miscellaneous lot. They were seventeen in number, and included two innkeepers and two beer retailers. There was also a vinegar dealer and a milkman. To-day the street is the centre of the local carrying trade; vans, lurries and carts travelling daily between the country districts on all sides of the city and the city—an industry which, in spite of the development of the railway system, is of great importance to the trading section of the community.

WITHY GROVE.

PART IV.

SOME NOTABLE RESIDENTS.

THOMAS BARRITT.

In attempting to piece together the numerous fragments that go to make up the history of our city, its streets, its institutions, and its builders, we are indebted to a number of persons who, in one way or another, have left records of their knowledge of the changes that have taken place in and before their time. Prominent amongst these is Thomas Barritt, who collected a large amount of information, brought together a fine collection of interesting relics, and left behind him a number of interesting sketches of the streets and buildings of the town as he knew it. A few generations ago it was deemed fashionable and regarded as a proof of superior education to sneer at such men and their work. To-day, thanks to the growth of a more tolerant spirit, the value of such work is becoming generally recognised. When Wheeler wrote his *History of Manchester* the former spirit prevailed, and it influenced him in describing Barritt and his work. He says of him: "In his day a most devoted disciple of antiquarianism—that dry and dusty science—was also a native of the town of

Manchester, in which he lived, died, was buried, and (we may almost add) has been forgotten."

He was born in a house that stood next door to the Roebuck Tavern that formerly stood in Hanging, Ditch. The tavern and the house were removed when Corporation Street was made. By trade a saddler, Barritt carried on business in several shops in Hanging Ditch and Withy Grove, never living many yards away from the place of his birth. We must bear in mind that in his day Withy Grove was semi-rural in its surroundings. His love of antiquities served as a hobby and a recreation, and in the intervals of a working life he collected not only a large amount of information concerning Manchester, but made a fine collection of old armour, stained glass, copies of ancient inscriptions, and drawings of old buildings. Many of his manuscripts, together with his scrap books were purchased by the feoffees of Chetham's College, where they may still be seen, his books were sold by auction ; his collection of stained glass and many of his pictures were purchased by Mr. W. Ford, the well-known bookseller, and the greater part of his old armour was bought by Mrs. Isherwood, of Marple Hall. He was an active member of the Literary and Philosophical Society. He was three times married. Owing to an accident he lost a leg early in life, and obtained a cork substitute. Although he received no education in childhood he became a fair scholar, and won for himself the respect of his fellow townsmen. He died October 29th, 1820, and was interred by torchlight, his funeral being "attended by thirty or forty of the most respectable of the inhabitants."

In this connection I can give an interesting reminiscence contributed by a subscriber to these volumes. In a letter in which she refers to her connection with Cheetwood, she says of the house in which she had lived : " The house we lived in once belonged to Parson Wray, of the Old Church, and he must have lived there at the time when part of the churchyard was taken away to make the road from Victoria Street to Hunt's Bank. He had a great many of the grave stones taken up to his house at Cheetwood, and then paved the yard with them (with the inscriptions showing). Our visitors would always ask if it had been a burial ground, but of course our people could explain how the stones came to be there. One gravestone I have read hundreds of times. It was 'Thomas Barritt, saddler,' with date of death. This was the famous Thomas Barritt. I daresay many will wonder where his grave was." Thus it comes about that the gravestone of he who had done so much to preserve the record of our city's history has been lost ; for the gravestones referred to have in more recent years been removed. The exact wording of the inscription has been lost, but the following lines, written by Joseph Aston, and printed on a memorial card, have survived :

" Here resteth the remains of Thomas Barritt, a profound antiquarian, and a good man. He died, honoured and respected by all ranks of society, October 29th, 1820, aged 77 years.

In Mancunium lived a man who knew
Much of old times, and much of ancient lore ;
Strange and scarce books had he, and curious coins,
Medals and painted glass, and ponderous arms ;
Helmets and breastplates, gauntlets vast, and shields
Of many kinds, proof against bloody war ;
Swords without number, of all murdering shapes,
And one, which erst had grac'd a prince's thigh,

More valued than the rest—and more rever'd
By him who owned it, and by all his friends,
He was vers'd in heraldry, and could tell
How all the thanes, and all the knights, and squires
Within his shire, had sprung from times remote.
And famed too, was he, for his industry;
For aye at work, for much his business called;
And yet full many a picture did he paint.
Pedigrees copied, branch and root, carvings made
Of antique shapes; and almost beyond belief,
Helmets and shields to rival Greece and Rome;
Stealing from sleep the time to give them form;
Nay once, grappling Patience, he made a suit of mail,
With thousand upon thousand links; for the love
He bore to ancient arms; for he was curious
As the searching air, which pries, without a blush,
In to things scarce, or sacred, or profane."

JAMES MURRAY.

A near neighbour of Thomas Barritt's was James Murray, who carried on the business of a confectioner at No. 2 Withy Grove. He became known to fame as a result of the part that he played in connection with the meetings of the Reformers prior to the holding of the Peterloo meetings on August 16th, 1819. The demand for parliamentary reform occupied the attentions of the working classes of Lancashire, but the Government of the day refused to move in the matter. A large number of small meetings had been held in the various parts of the county but without result; and as a result a large united gathering of reformers, to be held on St. Peter's field, was decided upon. Knowing that those who joined in demanding reform were usually described by their opponents as roughs and disorderly characters, it was decided, if possible, to remove any possible grounds there might be for such a charge. Cleanliness, sobriety and order were insisted upon by Bamford and other leaders; and it was decided that these should be maintained in their march to the place of meeting and during the meeting. This was to be secured by drilling, and at White Moss the reformers of the district met and were drilled by an old soldier. Their operations were watched by a number of Government spies, one of whom, James Murray, was seen and recognised by the reformers. A rush was made for him, and he was beaten by members of the crowd and was afterwards taken home in a vehicle. The fact that he went to the meeting disguised as a weaver justifies the statement that he went as a spy. So unpopular did he become as a result of his actions that his business as a confectioner gradually died out, and he retired upon a competency previously secured.

JOHN DOHERTY.

Another well-known character associated with Withy Grove was John Doherty, who having been born in 1797 at Buncrana, Inishowen, in the County of Donegal, found his way to Manchester about 1814 in search of a fortune. He obtained employment in a cotton mill and ultimately became a spinner. In those days cotton spinners earned better wages than obtained in any other branch of labour, and they formed themselves into an association or union. About 1830 Doherty left cotton spinning, and shortly afterwards edited a reform paper called *The Voice of the People*, the first number of which was issued on January 1st, 1831. Its life was only short. His next venture was *The Poor Man's Advocate*. The first four numbers had been issued from 24 Market Street by A. Wilkinson ; number five was printed and sold by Abel Heywood, and number six bears the name of W. Strange, 21 Paternoster Row. The seventh issue, dated March 3rd, 1832, bears as the imprint the announcement: "Printed and published by J. Doherty, 10 Boundary Street, Chorlton Row (until suitable premises can be obtained)" but on the 31st of the same month the address was changed to 37 Withy Grove, where Doherty had commenced business as a bookseller and printer. In the same number there appeared an article entitled "Clerical Resurrectionism," which involved Doherty in a prosecution for libel. The libel consisted in an allegation that the body of a Mr. Perry had been stolen from the grave yard of St. Thomas's Church, Stockport, with the knowledge of the incumbent, the Rev. Martin Gilpin, and that the body was conveyed to the dissecting room of Mr. Gilpin's brother-in-law, Mr. E. Lacy, a Manchester practitioner. The case was tried at the Lancaster assizes on August 29th, 1832, and Doherty was found guilty, and was sentenced to a month's imprisonment. A few months later he became involved in another case arising out of his journal. In this case he was charged with libelling Arrowsmith and Ogden, cotton spinners of Lees, near Oldham, but the case appears to have been abandoned.

The Poor Man's Advocate, as its title denotes, strongly advocated the cause of the operatives. Its life was stormy and brief. Doherty took an active part in the agitation that culminated in the passing through Parliament of the Ten Hours Bill, and was a member of the first committee formed to advance the proposed reform. As a dissenter he resisted the payment of Church rates, and on one occasion had his dining table seized and sold for non-payment. He also suffered imprisonment for selling unstamped newspapers. When he died in 1854 Lord Ashley, afterwards the Earl of Shaftesbury, writing to Philip Grant, said: "Poor Doherty was one of the most faithful to a cause that ever existed."

Before closing this brief reference to an earnest and strenuous worker for reform, I will make some reference to the work he carried on in Withy Grove. A woodcut of the shop may be seen amongst the advertisements in the *Manchester and Salford Advertiser* for March 2nd, 1833. The shop was described as "Doherty's London Periodical Office," and over it Doherty conducted the "Manchester Coffee News Room," where "ninety-six newspapers and publications may be seen every week." Most of these were sold at half price on the day before the publication of the succeeding number. A list of forty-four of these periodicals is given in the advertisement referred to The monthly and quarterly magazines were lent out to read on the arrival of the succeeding number, and the *Mirror of Parliament* was regularly filed. The charge for admission to the room was one penny. A cup of coffee (sugar and cream included) was obtainable for two pence; a basin of coffee, three pence; a pot of coffee, five pence; a cup of tea twopence halfpenny; a pot of tea, fivepence; bread and butter, a penny, roll and butter, twopence; toast and butter, threepence; and eggs, one penny each. Such were some of the charges made at the Withy Grove News Room more than seventy years ago.

Another resident in Withy Grove many years ago was a druggist named Mellor, who was usually called "Old Doctor Mellor." In the early volunteer days, more than a century ago, when the rendezvous of recruiting parties was the Seven Stars public house, he had the privilege of measuring and examining all the recruits enlisted in the town. As he received a fee for each case, and as some thousands of men must have passed through his hands, the privilege was one well worth having, and Mellor was proportionately envied by many of his less fortunate brethren of the pestle.

JACOB FRANCKS.

Seventy years ago, or thereabouts, Jacob Francks carried on business at 19 Withy Grove and at 25 St. Mary's Gate, as an optician and clothes dealer. This is a curious combination, but not so curious as that which was associated with his earlier place of business. This was at 4 Miller's Lane; and whilst there Francks published a business card, one copy of which has survived. It reads thus: "J. Francks, optician, 4 Miller's Lane, makes or repairs all sorts of optic glasses, telescopes, microscopes, and reading glasses, spectacles, Likewise excellent tooth powder. Also excellent eye-water. Excellent rhubarb. Umbrellas made and neatly mended. Mr. Francks was eleven years a prisoner with the savages in America. At the time he made his escape from them he was chief of one of their tribes. This plate was engraved by himself." Mr. Francks was evidently a man of resource, and did not confine his attention to one branch of trade. The name of Franks is still familiar to Manchester people, but the sale of clothing, toothpowder and eyewater, and the repair of umbrellas no longer remains a branch of the opticians' business.

Mr. Franck's neighbours in the street were all engaged in the retail trade, and resided on the premises, with the exception of Messrs. Joseph and Samuel Dobell, who carried on a wholesale trade as cheese factors at 14 Withy Grove, next door to the Seven Stars, which business is still carried on under the same name. It is notable that seventy years ago no fewer than five of the shops in the street were occupied by clothes dealers. Soon afterwards the change in the nature of the businesses carried on in the street commenced, and to-day the actual residents are remarkably few in number. The building of the *Sporting Chronicle* offices was an important event in the history of the thoroughfare, and to-day as the home of the *Evening Chronicle* and the *Daily Dispatch* it is well-known to thousands of persons in all parts of the country.

SHUDEHILL.

Part I.

Shudehill is another of our old street names concerning the origin of which there is much doubt. It has frequently been stated that it arose from the fact that many generations ago a mill stood on the higher lands, and that the shudes or husks being thrown down the hill side gave the name to the thoroughfare. This may have been so, but it is extremely doubtful, for not only have we no record of the existence of any such mill, but in the earliest days of our community it was usual to build mills upon the banks of rivers having a swift current. No such stream existed on Shudehill, for although a stream ran from the pits that formerly occupied a portion of the area, it would not be of sufficient power to turn the wheel of a corn mill. The origin of the name therefore remains a mystery.

One of the earliest references to Shudehill is in the Court Leet Records, wherein we read that on March 29th, 1554, James Chetam was ordered to "make the highway sufficient for carts to come and go." As showing the value of land in those days mention may be made of another entry in the records, under date 1566, wherein it states that Ellen Gillat was "heir for one parcel of land lying in Sude Hill, for which is paid 8d. by year unto the lord " (of the Manor); and four years later we find mention that Ralph Proudlove and his wife held a burgage " at a place called Suydehill and payeth thereof yearly to the lord 8d." The different modes of spelling street names in those early days arose from the fact that education was given to only a very limited degree, and each clerk was a law unto himself in the matter of spelling.

In 1597 there is an entry that is of interest as bearing upon a question dealt with in a previous volume. The jury ordered that " no person shall get any clay in the Withingreave in any part of the lane, till they come to the Shudehill, and not to get any in that lane within ten yards of the causeway." For a breach of this order the heavy penalty of five shillings was imposed. The matter was again mentioned at a meeting of the Court two years later when it was ordered that " No doobe nor clay shall be gotten between the Pinfold and the Shudehill." The penalty for breach of the order was fixed at three shillings and four pence, and a fortnight later a special officer was sworn in to see that the order was obeyed. The Pinfold stood until about a century ago at the top of Shudehill on a plot of land near to the corner of Rochdale Road then called Back Lane. In the days when pigs were turned into the street by careless owners, possibly under the care of a young child, any person finding a pig straying unattended would drive it to the Pinfold, and would receive one shilling, which sum the owner would be compelled to refund on claiming the animal.

On the 1650 plan of the town Shudehill is depicted as a country lane extending from the top of Withing

Grove to the corner of Miller's Lane. At the bottom, somewhere near to where the Rover's Return stands, stood a building. As no garden is depicted as being attached to it it is probable that the building was a barn connected with Withingreave Hall. The latter building probably stood a little lower down Withy Grove. This brings to mind a statement often made that the old inn of to-day at one time formed a portion of the out-buildings connected with Withingreave Hall. Some account of the Hall and one of its occupants will be given in the next chapter. Returning to our plan we find that the only other buildings in Shudehill two and a half centuries ago were two blocks of cottages on the opposite side of the lane. Each seems to have consisted of three tenements with gardens attached. In the course of the next century the whole of the street as far as the corner of Miller's Lane was built up, although the back land behind the houses remained open. Very little building seems to have taken place on the opposite site and the whole of the space now represented by the market was a large field, the boundary on the one side being marked by a hedge dividing it from Shudehill.

IN 1794.

By 1794 still further changes had been made, for Hanover Street had been almost completely built up, a few open spaces only remaining between the rows of better class houses of which the street was formed. Bradshaw Street, Snow Hill, Cold House, and other adjacent streets had lost their rural appearance. On the opposite side of Shudehill some building had been done, Copperas Street, Edge Street and Thomas Street, together with Coop Street and Oak Street, together with some minor streets having been made. Much of the land now occupied by the market had been converted into gardens belonging very probably to some of the residents in the adjacent streets. What is now known as Swan Street is marked on Laurent's plan as New Cross Street, from the new market cross that had been erected at the top of Oldham Street. Along the Rochdale Road side of New Cross Street were the pieces of water known as the Shudehill pits, and behind them were more gardens in many of which there seems to have been summer houses. A century ago the district round about the upper end of Shudehill could fairly lay claim to be regarded as being in the country.

The Shudehill pits were converted into reservoirs, from which the town received a portion of its water supply, by Sir Oswald Mosley, towards the close of the eighteenth century. The water was raised from the river Medlock at Holt Town by means of a pumping engine, and was conveyed by pipes to the Shudehill pits and to the infirmary pond. This was Manchester's principal water supply until 1826 when a reservoir was formed at Gorton. A change was made in 1808, but it only consisted in making a reservoir at Holt Town from whence the water ran to Piccadilly; and strange as it may appear to us, Manchester, a century ago, obtained its water for culinary purposes from the river Medlock.

When the Holt Town reservoir was made the Shudehill pits were partly filled up and buildings were erected on the site. One of the first of these was a Wesleyan

Chapel, which was intended to relieve the pressure on the Oldham Street Chapel, which was filled to overflowing at every service. In 1823 the chapel, for reasons which have not been recorded, was converted into houses and shops, and to-day it is occupied by the premises of Messrs. Hargreaves, tobacco manufacturers.

In closing the references to the Shudehill pits a copy of an advertisement which appeared in *Whitworth's Manchester Magazine* on July 30th, 1765 may be, reproduced, supplying as it does an interesting glimpse of one phase of town life in those days. The announcement ran :—

" Whereas, the Reservoir at the top of Shudehill was by some malicious person cut down, and the water let off, on the 13th of this month. This is therefore to give notice, that if any person will inform who did the same, they shall upon conviction of the offender receive five guineas reward. And whereas some persons have made a practice of drowning cats and dogs, washing dirty linen, and carrying away water from Shude Hill pits, and the pit at the top of Market Street Lane, without consent ; This is therefore to give notice, that if any person or persons do the same for the future, they shall be prosecuted to the utmost rigour of the law."

SHUDEHILL.

Part II.

COLDHOUSE CHAPEL AND BRADSHAW HALL.

On the evening of March 10th, 1899, a meeting of trustees and others interested in the Coldhouse Baptist Chapel, Thorniley Brow, was held to consider the question of the proposed chapel to be erected at Didsbury. The Coldhouse Chapel was situated off a narrow street, and the visitor to it had to grope his way to it through a narrow passage, in the middle of which there was a short flight of stairs. The little building had outlived its time, and for twelve years it had been closed. About a dozen persons met in the chapel, which presented a cheerless and forlorn appearance. The forms were thick with dust, the windows had been broken, and light was obtained by means of a few candles stuck into bottles. The meeting decided to accept an offer of £550 for the building, the proceeds being applied to the purchase of a piece of land at Didsbury, whereon to build a Baptist Chapel and School. Such was the concluding chapter in an interesting record.

The story may be said to have dated back to that Black Bartholomew's Day, Sunday, August 24th, 1662, whereon two thousand ministers were ejected from their livings for refusing to accept the Act of Uniformity.

One of these was the Rev. Henry Newcome, who was a Fellow of the Collegiate Church. When Charles II. issued his declaration of Indulgence in 1671 Newcome obtained a license to preach and conduct service in his own dwelling. A month later he also secured permission to preach in a barn that stood in the Cold-house meadow, Shudehill, and began to hold services there. There was much opposition on the part of the Church adherents, who on one occasion secured a warrant for the preacher's apprehension, and he was taken before the magistrates, only to be released. After a time the services were removed from the barn, which had been fitted to serve as a chapel, to Mr. Newcome's house ; and in 1676 the furniture was removed from the barn. He continued to conduct services at private houses, until James II.'s Declaration of Indulgence appeared in April, 1687, when, owing to the increase in the number of the congregation, a removal was made back to the barn, which was extended and refurnished. Services were held there until the meeting house in Pool Fold, now known as the Cross Street Chapel, was opened. The barn chapel then fell into disuse, and was not used regularly for the holding of services until about 1749, when the Methodists, who had commenced operations in a garrett off Deansgate, found it necessary to build a chapel. The number of worshippers had increased to such an extent that the Thorniley Brow Chapel was used until the new building in Birchin Lane was ready for occupation. It is said that the barn chapel had been rebuilt before the Methodists took possession of it. The next tenants were the Independents, whose minister, the

Rev. Caleb Warhurst, commenced holding services there in 1751. So great was his popularity as a preacher that the building was enlarged in 1756, and five years later the building of the Cannon Street Chapel was commenced. The little building, again deserted, was next tenanted by the Baptists, in whose possession it remained until the date of the sale to which reference has already been made. For more than a century services were held within its walls, although it never seems to have been very prosperous. The minister there a century ago was the Rev. J. Bruce; but soon afterwards the chapel ceased to have a minister of its own, and services were conducted by laymen and occasionally by preachers connected with other chapels.

There was at one time a small burial ground behind the chapel, and in August, 1874, in the course of excavations there, six coffins were unearthed. The lids of the coffins were very curiously inscribed with figures and initials formed of steel nails. The dates ranged from 1770 to 1774. Such in brief is the record, so far as it is known, of an old-world place of worship, which, having originally been built when the land thereabouts was devoted to farming purposes, saw such changes in its surroundings that ultimately no reason remained to justify its continuance.

BRADSHAW HALL.

Hidden away behind the buildings that face into Nicholas Croft, and standing between Bradshaw Street and Snow Hill stands Bradshaw Hall, once the home of a well-known family, but now quite forgotten. Formerly there stood in front of it a piece of garden ground, the boundary wall of which was in Shudehill. More than a century ago that land was covered with houses, which in later years were converted into shops. To-day the building is used for business purposes, although its handsome front, the fine old oaken staircase, the oak shutters, and some of the old windows remain to remind us what a fine residence it was a century and a half ago. The most notable resident who ever lived there was John Bradshaw, who for a long period of years was an active magistrate, and took a leading part in town affairs. He was born in 1708, and at the age of twenty-five was placed on the commission of the peace. In 1753 he was high sheriff of the county, and four years later the neighbourhood of Shudehill was the scene of much excitement.

SHUDEHILL FIGHT.

During the years 1753-7 there had been a general scarcity and dearness of food, and in consequence there was general discontent. In several cases that discontent took the form of food riots. The first of these took place on June 6th, 1757, when the mob seized the provisions brought to the Shudehill market. The succeeding harvest brought no alleviation of the sufferings of the poor, and discontent increased until on November 15 it culminated in a riot. An account of this occurrence was published at the time on a broadside, a copy of which has survived. The following is a verbatim copy of the contents of the document. At the head of the sheet, under the heading "The account of the riot at Shudehill," is a crude representation of soldiers armed with lances or spears and guns; under which is the description of the encounter.

"On Saturday about nine hundred rioters came from Clayton, after destroying the corn mills there. A party of soldiers was ordered by the High Sheriff to Shudehill to be ready for them. About eleven o'clock they came up, and pelted the soldiers with stones by which one was killed and nine wounded; in return for which the soldiers fired on them, and killed three and wounded fifteen, who were taken to the infirmary. Two hours after that they assembled again, and went to Bramhall's Mills, near the town, and destroyed the House Mills, and burnt the haystacks. At night a part of them returned to the town and attempted to break open the dungeon on Salford Bridge, and release a rioter that was confined there. In order to prevent a second riot the constables released him. Besides those killed in the fray, a fine young man, a son of Mr. Newton, was shot. He had climbed a tree to see the riot." Such was a contemporaneous account of the affair that was afterwards known as the "Shudehill Fight."

Mr. Bradshaw, in conjunction with Mr. Bailey, of Withington, a relative by marriage, and who was High Sheriff at the time, took an active part in quelling the disturbances. Tim Bobbin published a lengthy account of the incident in the form of a pamphlet bearing the title of *Truth in a Mask, or the Shudehill Fight*. John Bradshaw married Elizabeth, youngest daughter of the Rev. Samuel Peploe, Bishop of Chester, and Warden of the Collegiate Church of Manchester. His son, James, in later years resided at Darcy Lever; and of his two daughters, Ann married Charles White, the well-known Manchester surgeon, whose house stood on the site of the Reference Library, King Street; and Elizabeth married Radcliffe, son of the Rev. Samuel Sidebottom, of Middleton. John Bradshaw is frequently mentioned in Dr. Byrom's letters. He died in 1777 and was buried in the Collegiate Church. His name appears in the Manchester directories for 1772 and 1773. After his death the mansion appears to have remained untenanted for some time. Early in the last century it was occupied by Stephen Sheldon, who is described in the directories as being a grocer of 20 Shudehill, but whose house was next door to the shop or number 21, tenements being numbered consecutively and not alternately as is the custom to-day. In 1836 Sheldon's business had been removed to Swan Street, but the old premises were occupied by another grocer, Robert Jones. At that time, owing to re-numbering, the front premises had become number 41. Since then the old residence and the buildings built on the garden have been occupied for business purposes by a succession of tenants, but nothing further has occurred in connection with it worthy of record.

W.&A. CROMPTON.

SHUDEHILL.

PART III.

WITHINGREAVE HALL AND WILLIAM HULME, THE FOUNDER.

One of the few remaining relics of ancient Shudehill is the quaint black and white building known as "The Rover's Return." If tradition speaks truly in the matter the house is even more interesting on account of its associations, for we are told that several centuries ago it formed a portion of the outhouses connected with Withingreave Hall, the town residence of the Hulme family, to one of whom Manchester is so much indebted in the matter of education. Before going further it will be as well to pause for a moment to draw attention to Manchester's four great educational founders. They comprise Hugh Oldham, the founder of the Grammar School; Humphrey Chetham, the founder of the charity bearing his name; John Owens, the founder of Owens College, out of which has been evolved the Manchester University; and William Hulme, the founder of the great Hulme Charity. Few towns or cities can boast of such a quartette of educational founders, and it was particularly appropriate that the city should be made the seat of a university.

There is nothing to show us when Withingreave Hall was built, who built it, nor its extent. Nor do we know the exact site occupied by it, nor when it was pulled down. Suffice it to say that it was one of the residences of William Hulme, who died on January 2nd, 1637. The family must have been one of good social position for in the inventory of William Hulme's goods and chattels we find that one portion of them were at his house called Hulme, in Redish, a second portion at his house at Outwood, in the parish of Prestwich, and a third portion at his house called Withingreave Hall, within the town of Manchester. He left only one child, a son William, who having been born on September 16th, 1631, was only five years old at the time of his father's death. By his will dated December 20th, 1636, the father appointed John Hulme, his younger brother, to be his son's guardian until he should reach the age of twenty-one.

William Hulme received his education at the Manchester Grammar School, and it is probable that he spent the greater part of his school days at Withingreave Hall. He married in 1653, Elizabeth, daughter of Ralph Robinson, of Kersley, and by her had one son, Banister, who died during his father's lifetime. William Hulme died on October 26, 1691, and was buried in the chapel founded by his ancestors in the Collegiate Church. The family had originally been connected with Reddish, then a portion of the ancient parish of Manchester. As far back as 1290 we read of Robert, son of William de Hulme, who conveyed certain lands there to Richard de Hull. The ancient home of the Hulmes stood on the site of the present Hulme or Broadstone Hall in Broadstone Road. The family founded a chapel in the Collegiate Church. It was situated on the south side of the building, adjacent to the Jesus Chantry. Having fallen to decay the chapel was rebuilt in 1810. It was here that the great founder was buried, and forty years ago a mutilated slab could be seen bearing the arms of the Hulme family together with the inscription : " William Hulme, of Hulme, Esq., buried, October ye 29th, 1691, æt suæ 61." Amidst the restorations the building has undergone the chapel has disappeared, and there is nothing to show where William Hulme was buried.

Such are the brief particulars known concerning the life of the founder who, in his will, after providing for his widow, left certain fields and meadows in trust to maintain as exhibitioners " four of the poorest sort of batchelors of arts taking such degree in Brazenose College in Oxford, as from time to time should resolve to continue, and reside there by the space of four years, next after such degree taken, to be nominated and approved of by the Warden of the Collegiate Church of Manchester, the rectors of the parish churches of Prestwich and Bury, for the time being, and their successors for ever." The widow survived for nearly nine years, dying in 1700. The remainder of the estate reverted to the charity after her death. At the time of Hulme's death the income of the charity was about £64 per annum, which allowed a payment of £16 each to the four batchelors of arts. Such was the modest foundation on which has been erected one of the greatest of our local educational charities. As the town grew land values increased, and to-day the modest income of £64 per annum is represented by many thousands of pounds. It will be observed that the distribution of the charity was left in the hands of three clergymen, although the will contains no reference to the teaching of religion. As the value of the property increased in value, and the income grew, it was necessary from time to time to obtain the sanction of Parliament to various changes. In 1770 an Act of Parliament was obtained by the trustees to enable them to grant building leases of lands belonging to the Charity, situated within the town of Manchester, for terms not exceeding ninety-nine years, or for one, two, or three lives. Power was also given to increase the number of exhibitioners from four to ten, whose stipends should never be less than £60 nor more than £80 per annum. By a further Act of Parliament, passed in 1795, powers were granted to the trustees to convey in fee or to grant leases for lives, or for long terms of years, with or without covenants for renewal, under reserved yearly rents. They were also empowered to increase the number of exhibitioners to fifteen, and the annual allowance to each exhibitioner to be £110.

In 1814 a private Act was passed, entitled: "An Act for amending two several Acts relating to the estates devised by William Hulme, Esq., and to enable the trustees thereof to apply the trust moneys in making an allowance to, and provision for, the exhibitioners of certain exhibitions founded by the testator for Brazenose College, Oxford, and also in founding and supporting a lecture in Divinity in the said college; and to incorporate the trustees, and for other purposes therein mentioned." At this time the annual proceeds of the trust estate amounted to £2502 16s. 8d. over and above the interest of the sum of £23,700 which the trustees had saved out of the rents and profits of the estates. By this Act the trustees were empowered to make a departure from the testator's directions by nominating undergraduates as exhibitioners a year before taking the degree of B.A. They were also empowered to allow to each exhibitioner an annual sum not exceeding £220 per annum.

In 1827 the trustees had again recourse to Parliament. By this time the annual income amounted to £4950 16s. 11d., and the savings to £42,203. They asked Parliament to enable them "to apply part of the present and future accumulations of the said trust estates and moneys in the purchase of advowsons of livings, and to present thereto such individuals as at the time of the avoidance of such livings actually should be, or theretofore should have been, exhibitioners on the foundation of the said testator in Brazenose College." The application does not seem to have excited opposition, or even to have attracted any degree of public attention, and thus an Act was quietly passed by which the powers sought for were conceded. But it was provided that a surplus fund should always be left of at least £20,000, and that no more than £7000 should be expended on any one advowson or benefice. Twelve years later, in 1839, the trustees appear to have thought that it was time to clench the nail which had been so cleverly driven thus far, but now they asked and obtained the following enactments, 2 Vict. c 171:—

(1) "The repeal of so much of the Statute 8 Geo. IV. as directed that the accumulated fund should be

kept up to £20,000, and the substitution of a proviso that the accumulation should not be less than £5000, and the consent of three-fourths of the trustees being first obtained in writing. Wanting such consent the limit was fixed at £10,000. (2) Power to endow or augment the endowment of any benefices purchased by the trust to an amount not exceeding £7000. (3) Power to expend such sums, not exceeding £7000 in each case, as they shall think fit, in building or endowing churches and chapels; to purchase or build parsonage houses at a cost not exceeding £700 in any one case; and to possess as patron all the rights possessed by the patron of any the like benefice."

Under the Act the trustees had, up to the year 1855, purchased twenty-nine benefices, the annual aggregate value of which appears to be about £5400. Every step that had been thus taken involved an unjustifiable departure from the testator's intent, and a gross perversion of the interest of the public in the endowment. The testator expressly says that he "desires to assist the *poor sort* of graduates whilst they are at College, and *no longer*." Under this system, we are told, "rich men degraded themselves by seeking for their sons, or dependent relations, a College education of seven years' duration, at the expense of a charity intended for poor scholars, and the trustees further tempted them to make the perversion coextensive with their lives." Thus what might have been a noble educational provision for men who have to fight the battle of life at a disadvantage, became but an additional cushion for men who were already at ease. An endowment which produced in half a century more than £200,000, educated during that time only about two hundred and eighty persons. The amount set apart for the purchase of advowsons from 1827 to 1839 was £46,546.

In 1851, after repeated attempts in preceding years, John Bright, in his place in the House of Commons, moved and carried a resolution for a " return in a tabular form, showing the several advowsons or ecclesiastical benefices purchased by or lately belonging to the Trustees of Mr. Hulme, the date when they were respectively purchased, the price paid for each, the gross annual income of each, the names of the present incumbents, and when such incumbents were respectively nominated or presented, and by whom." The return ordered was never made, and the then Home Secretary, Mr. Spencer Walpole, appears to have approved the refusal. After such approval from a Minister of State, it can scarcely excite surprise to find the President of Brazenose (Dr. Harrington) replying to a Royal Commission of Inquiry, appointed with the full knowledge and virtual approval of Parliament, that " the College declines to give information to parties with the object of whose inquiries they are unacquainted, and for whose authority to inquire they can find no warrant either in the Statutes of their Founders or in their Charter of Incorporation." The Royal Commission who were thus contemptuously treated included the distinguished Savilian, Professor of Geometry in the University of Oxford, the Master of Pembroke, the Dean of Carlisle, and that excellent and truly venerable prelate, the Bishop of Norwich.

For several years the administration of the trust gave rise to much public discussion, until at length the Queen in Council on August 26th, 1881, approved a scheme of the Charity Commissioners for the re-settlement of the foundation by providing a governing body which should be largely representative, to whom power was given to found new schools in Manchester, Oldham, and Bury, and a Hall of Residence for Church of England students attending Owens College. The Hulme Grammar School, Withington, was opened in 1887, and at a latter date schools at Bury and Oldham. In addition to other payments out of funds, sums of £1000 are annually made to the Manchester and Bury Schools, £1250 to the Oldham Grammar School, and grants are made to the Girls' High School, the Manchester University, and the Hulme Hall of Residence. The trustees now grant twenty exhibitions of £80 a year each, and they are the patrons of twenty-eight livings. The patronage of all livings belonging to the trust is vested in eleven trustees. The trust estate is in the hands of seven managers appointed in pursuance of the provisions of the scheme of 1881. The administration of the charity is in the hands of a board of governors, three of whom, the Dean of Manchester and the rectors of Bury and Prestwich, are ex-officio, and fifteen representatives nominated by various public bodies.

History says nothing as to the later residents of Withingreave Hall; but the following advertisement which appeared in *Whitworth's Manchester Magazine* in September, 1763, is not without interest. "To be sold, all that messuage and tenement, with the out-housing, orchard and garden, called Withingreave Hall, Also, one dwelling house, divided into three cottages.

And also four closes of land and meadow ground, containing eight acres and a half, lying very conveniently at the higher end of Shudehill."

SHUDEHILL.

PART IV.

SHUDEHILL AS A FARMING DISTRICT, AND ITS LATER HISTORY.

It is difficult to realise how at any time Shudehill could have been a country district, but I purpose in this chapter reproducing some details as to the tenancies in the district held under the Hulme trustees in 1710. We are told in the columns of the *Manchester Mercury* for 1785 that partridges were caught in the fields of Shudehill in the autumn of that year.

The rent roll referred to is headed as follows: "A rent roll of the Lands and Hereditaments devised in Trust by Wm. Hulme, late of Kersley, Esq., deceased for the use or benefit of four Batchelors of Arts in Brazenose College in Oxford, and the terms in being of such parts thereof as are in lease, and the rents and reservacons due by such leases, and also of such parts as are held at rack rents as rented in the year 1710. Likewise the number of acres belonging to the several tennements." Then follows the list from which the following extracts are made:—

"Mr. James Hilton; Withingreave Hall, outhousing, croft, orchard, and garden. a barne at Shudehill now converted into cottages; 4 closes of lande about 8 acres in lease from Xmas 1708, for 21 years .. 22 0 0

" Richard Gimney ; for Boarhead House, Backside and 4 stables, at Hidecross, one barn and cottages and about 4 acres of land in 2 closes in Newton Lane	20	0	0
" Richard Hopwood ; one house, 2 stables and coach house, with a garden at Hidecross, 3 closes nere Shudehill, one croft by Shudehill or Withingreave Hall, 5 acres one quarter, leased from Xmas, 1708, for 21 years	8	0	0
" Widow Shuttleworth ; cottages and smithy at Hidecross, leased from Xmas, 1708, for 21 years..	1	15	11

Widdow Leese leased a house in Fennell Street at £1 15s. 0d. a year ; John Lawton a cottage in Toad Lane for 16s. 0d. Edmund Neil, two houses in Fennell Street for £9 ; John Smith, a cottage in Shudehill for 8s. ; Isaac Bradshaw, a cottage and outhousing at Shudehill for £1 ; " Rachel Berron, Widdow," a cottage at Shudehill for 8s., and other tenants occupied similar tenements at similarly low rentals. The idea of renting eight acres of land together with a mansion and out-buildings for £22 a year is incomprehensible to us ; and gives us some idea of the tremendous rise that has taken place in land values.

One other item should be mentioned. Mr. Joseph Barlow leased two crofts at " Topp of Deansgate," for which he paid two shillings a year rent. In a footnote we are told : " Take notice, that one of the crofts Mr. Barlow has should lye to his Houseing and to the High Lane at top of Deansgate, and though it be separated now by a fence, yet that waste part belongs to the croft and not to Mr. Barlow's land." The land held by Mr. Barlow is now represented by a portion of Brazenose Street, Hulme Street, and the buildings thereabouts. A footpath formerly led through the fields from the Market Place to the land and possibly to Mr. Barlow's house. The footpath survives, a portion of it being represented by Exchange Street and St. Ann's Square, and a further portion by the passage running from King Street in continuation of St. Ann's Passage.

THE MARKET.

From farming to the sale of farm produce is but a step, and having referred to our thoroughfare in the farming days, let us now turn our attention to the institution by which it is better known to more persons of the present generation than for any other reason—the market.

For more than a century Shudehill has been a marketing centre, for Aston tells us that about 1804 the wholesale potato market was removed from Shudehill to Campfield, Deansgate, which new market was to be called St. John's Market. He then goes on to say that "Notwithstanding the major part of the potatoes brought into Manchester come into town within a few yards of this new market, yet the farmers are with difficulty prevailed to stop in it, but having paid the legal toll to the lord of the manor, proceed a mile further, to the old market, to meet their old customers upon the accustomed place of sale." In those days the cattle market was held at Hyde's Cross, the pig market being higher up the street. The attempt to remove the potato market was a failure, and in a few years the idea was abandoned. At that time the market was held in the street, but in 1820 a piece of land was purchased, and was used for the purpose. The right of holding markets and collecting market tolls was vested in the lord of the manor. In March, 1845, the town council decided to purchase the rights for the sum of £200,000. On several occasions since then the corporation have had recourse to the law courts to protect the rights thus secured. In 1876 they obtained an injunction against certain persons who had in effect set up a rival market, and a year later they obtained one restraining a potato dealer from selling wholesale in a cellar in Shudehill, near the market. In 1883 a decision was given in another case which had a most important effect upon the method of managing the market, for it was decided that the corporation were not entitled to charge tenants toll on the goods sold in addition to a rent charge. By reason of gradual extension the Shudehill Market has increased until now it covers an area of 26,212 square yards, and with the possible exception of London is the most extensive in the country. The wholesale potato market is now in Oldham Road.

The Smithfield or Shudehill Market, although of such great extent, is not the only property managed by the Markets Committee. The others vary in size from the "Hen Market" in Shudehill, and the Rising Sun Market, to the Abattoirs and Carcase Market, and the Foreign Animals Wharf. In all, the properties of the Committee cover an area of over 137,000 square yards, which together with all footpaths and passages connected with them, extend to 28½ acres. The whole shows a remarkable development since 1845, for when the corporation took the market over they were small in area, and in several cases the public streets were used for the purpose, much inconvenience to ordinary traffic being caused thereby.

A FEW FAMILIAR NAMES.

Beyond the names already mentioned few of the persons who have been associated with Shudehill have achieved more than a very local reputation. Of the small minority several have been already dealt with in other connection in earlier volumes. These include Thomas Fildes, the pioneer of Sunday Schools in Manchester; or to speak perhaps more correctly, one of three pioneers of the London Road Sunday School.

Joseph Johnson, who carried on business as a brush maker at 17 Shudehill, ninety years ago, took a leading part in the reform agitation that may be said to have culminated in the passing of the first Reform Bill. He was present at Peterloo, and was afterwards imprisoned for twelve months for the part he took in the meeting. As in the cases of the other "politicals" his sentence was rigorously carried out. Whilst he was in prison he asked permission to visit his wife's death bed in the custody of prison officials, which permission was refused. In later years he denounced Henry Hunt as a conceited, notoriety hunter, and in 1822 published in pamphlet form an open letter which he addressed: "To Saint Henry of Ilchester."

Bamford, in his *Passages in the Life of a Radical* noticed with commendation Johnson's sturdy and pithy defence at his trial, and compared it with the longwinded and ineffective speech made by Hunt. After the prisoners had been released a sum of money that had been collected for the purpose, was invested in the purchase of annuities for Hunt, Johnson, and Cobbett, with reversion to the survivors in case of death of the other. Johnson was the survivor and until his death in 1872 he received the triple annuity. Towards the close of his life Johnson's political opinions changed very considerably, and for some years before his death he was a Conservative of a very pronounced type. He died at Northenden on September 5th, 1872, in his eighty-second year.

A century ago Peel and Williams's foundry stood near to the Shudehill pits. The Phoenix Foundry was commenced very early in the century by George Peel whose father, Joseph Peel, was uncle to the first Sir Robert Peel. He had originally been a reed maker and iron founder in Halliwell Street, Long Millgate, but being joined by William Williams, the firm branched out and put up an extensive foundry at Shudehill. Peel married Rebecca, daughter of Richard Barlow, of Stand, by whom he had two sons, Joseph Peel, of Singleton Brook, who took an active part in the volunteer movement, and George Peel, who in addition to being a good business man, had literary and artistic tastes. He was a governor of the Royal Institution, and one of the early members of the Chetham Society. He is described as having been a very "clubable" man. The firm after the father's death built the Soho Foundry, Pollard Street, Ancoats, where for many decades as Peel, Williams and Peel, they carried on a very extensive business in boilers and engines.

It should be placed on record that the noted balloonist, Mr. Sadler, made an ascent on June 29th, 1812 from a ropewalk that stood immediately behind Peel and Williams' foundry at Shudehill.

Mention has been made of the Fildes family who kept a grocer's shop at 40 Shudehill, and who in various ways took a prominent part in the town life of bygone days. Next door to their shop was the druggist's shop of G. H. Winder, whose son became a medical man of some repute in the town. Winder's business was afterwards taken over by Joseph Brooks, who had served his apprenticeship with Samuel Buckley, who had a druggist's shop at 233 Deansgate. The shop stood at the corner of Fleet Street, on a site now represented by the goods station yard. Mr. Brooks commenced business on his own account at Shudehill in 1851, in premises very much smaller than the present building. In 1882 he entered the City Council for Collegiate Ward, and some years later was appointed Chairman of the Waterworks' Committee. In other ways he rendered valuable services to the city, and by his death the city lost a conscientious worker.

Another resident of Shudehill for many years was Matthew Thackray, who carried on business as a bookseller. He had served some years in the boot and shoe trade with T. Thompson, whose shoe warehouse was at 35 Withy Grove. He first commenced business as a bookseller at 61 Shudehill. Afterwards, having built two shops in the same thoroughfare, numbered 51 and 53, he removed to the former one, and let the other one to Thomas Rushworth. It is interesting to note that each one had a son who has taken a prominent part in our local municipal affairs. Matthew Thackray's son, Edward, born at the Shudehill shop, after being educated at Rain's school, the Manchester Grammar School, and the Mechanics' Institution, entered the employment of the corporation as a clerk in the Treasurer's office. That was in 1859, and to-day Mr. Thackray occupies the responsible post of City Treasurer, having been appointed to the position when Mr. W. Martin resigned in 1897.

Thomas Rushworth represented Collegiate Ward in the Council from 1846 to 1857, and his example was copied by his son, James, who entered the Council as a representative for Cheetham Ward in 1880, and was promoted to the Aldermanic bench in 1892.

ROCHDALE ROAD.

Part I.

COLLYHURST COMMON.

In opening the story of Rochdale Road, which is certainly not one of the most delightful roads into the city, it will be as well to say something concerning Collyhurst, because long before Rochdale Road as such was known, in the days which it was nothing more than a minor country lane, one district through which it passes was of first importance to the burgesses of Manchester. In those days Back Lane, as Rochdale Road was called a century ago, probably did not exist, or if it did exist, it was nothing more than a footpath or possibly an occupation road leading to the common land at Collyhurst which was usually approached by way of Long Millgate and Ashley Lane. We must therefore endeavour to imagine ourselves on a large tract of open land on which the burgesses of the town had the right of pasturage. The country round about would very probably be tilled by farmers, and five hundred years ago there would not exist any sign that would point to the complete change that has come over that district in the last century and a half. Collyhurst was then a quiet country place, with few residents, situated about a mile and a half from the little town that clustered around the Collegiate Church of Manchester.

First let us glance at the name, noting its probable origin and some of the ways in which it was spelled by our forefathers. Harland suggests that the name is derived from two Anglo Saxon words, col, meaning a peak or sharp hillock, and hyrst, meaning a wooded place; or that it is a corruption of Cadwall or Cold-wall-hurst. In the matter of ancient spelling few local names offer so many varieties, culled from deeds and other ancient documents. Thus we have Colihurst in an undated deed, Colahurst and Colyhurst in 1322, Cole-hurst in 1459, Colyers in 1553, Colyhurst Fould in 1556, Colyhurste in 1558, Colihurste in 1596, Collihurst in 1603, Colly hurst in 1611, and Colly-hurst foote in 1626, and others. Then we have mention of the Quarry and Four Lane ends in 1651; and Walke Lane and Four Lane Ends in 1666.

The common at Collyhurst had probably been regarded as common land from the time of the settlement after the victory of the Normans. Whether such was the case, or whether it was the result of later action we know that originally an area representing about eighty acres and including a large proportion of forest land was, five hundred years ago, unenclosed and open to be used by the burgesses of Manchester for pasturage. The natural inclination of the landowner to add to his possessions by enclosing and taking possession of common lands was illustrated in 1574, when the lord of the manor, William West, seventeenth Baron of Mamecestre, enclosed the common of Collyhurst, but his enclosure was "put downe the same night." Hollinworth in his Mancuniensis says that after this repulse he attempted as a compromise to "lett to such as choose to give for it four shillings, the aker by yeares, and twenty shillings fine aforehand." In a later generation Sir Nicholas Mosley, lord of the manor, made another attempt to enclose the common, for which he was paid 6s. 4d. annual rental. His action was resisted by William Radcliffe, of Radcliffe Hall, and other principal inhabitants, who commenced legal proceedings against him in the Duchy Court. Before the case was settled Sir Nicholas died, and was succeeded in his estates by Rowland Mosley, who obtained a settlement highly satisfactory to himself. He and his heirs were to be allowed to enclose and hold the land, and the right of common pasturage by the burgesses was to be rescinded. Six acres of the land nearest to the town was however to be reserved for the use of the burgesses, who when any epidemic or plague should break out in the town, would be free to erect cabins for the relief and isolation of infected persons, and to bury the victims who succumbed. In return for this concession Rowland Mosley agreed to pay a yearly rental of £10 for the use of the poor of Manchester for ever, the same to be paid out of the said Collyhurst land at Lady Day and Michaelmas. This rent charge has been paid regularly to successive boroughreeves of the town, and since the incorporation of Manchester, to the Mayor. The date of the settlement was 1607.

Reverting now to the Court Leet records, let us see how our forefathers used their right of pasturage prior to that date. At a meeting of the Court held on December 11th, 1534, the jury ordered "that the inhabitants of the town of Manchester that doth keep swyne, shall pay unto an officer that shall be paid to keep them upon a common called Colyers, for every swyne quarterly one penny ; or so to keep them within upon their backside, that they do not go abroad in town or market, or in churchyard." Most of the inhabitants kept pigs in those days, and although they had the right of pasturage or feeding them in the lord's woods it was a somewhat serious undertaking to drive them there for the purpose. It was much easier to let them roam about the streets and lanes of the little town, and about the market place and the churchyard, picking up such garbage and refuse that they found. In time this custom became so general as to become a nuisance, and the Court Leet passed the order quoted, and at the same time appointed a swine herd, whose duty it was to pass through the town each morning, blowing a horn so that the burgesses might turn their pigs out. Having collected his charges the herd conducted them by Ashley Lane to Collyhurst, where he remained till evening, when he returned leaving the members of his flock with their respective owners. For these services he was paid at fourpence per year, payable quarterly, for each pig, a rate of payment certainly nor erring in the direction of extravagance, even considering the increased value of money in those days.

Although this matter was frequently brought to the attention of the Court Leet, burgesses seem to have been very lax in their observance of the orders of the court. The consequence was that in 1560 the following more drastic order was passed. "Whereas at the last Court it was ordered that no swine should come abroad into the street, etc., the premises whereof standing they go abroad still; whereof we further order that after the feast of St. Martin there shall no swine go into the street, unless they be both ringed and yoked; and that to be when they drive them of necessity unto Collyhurst or some convenient place, and there leave them until evening that they come unto their houses again, for every swine 2d. And that the same shall be duly observed we appoint these persons (five in number) to see the same duly executed and observed." The twopence referred to was the amount of fine to be imposed for infringement of the order. In 1566 the fine was raised to fourpence; but in 1568 it was still further increased to five shillings; and thirteen burgesses were appointed to see that the order was carried out. In 1570 Thomas Ranshawe was appointed town swine-herd, with the intimation that if he failed to carry out his duties another appointment was to be made by the constables. These are specimens of many entries to be found in our Court Leet records concerning the feeding of swine on the common lands of Collyhurst.

The Court on several occasions had before them complaints of persons other than burgesses grazing their cattle; and in 1561 it was found necessary to impose a heavy fine on such offenders.

In view of the fact that prior to 1618 the lord of the manor had without consent of the Court Leet enclosed some thirty out of the eighty acres of waste land at Collyhurst, the following entry in the record of the proceedings of the Court for April 9th, 1556, is somewhat curious. "The jury doth find that Richard Radcliffe or his tenant hath encroached the lord's waste at Colyhurste Foold; and further the jury doth order that the said Richard, or his tenant there, shall make the hedge in the old place, and lay down the said encroachment to the common as it hath been heretofore." It is very evident that although the lord of the manor might enclose common land, no one else was permitted to do so.

Land grabbing would appear to have become common at Collyhurst in 1602, for another entry reads thus: "Divers encroachments have been made since the last Court Leet upon the common of Colehurste, where the burgesses of Manchester have free common of pasture, without stint of number; by means of which enclosures the Queen's tenants, burgesses and inhabitants of Manchester be greatly damnified; ordered that all those that have so enclosed, shall lay all such open before 10th May next. And that no person shall hereafter make any enclosure or encroachment upon the waste ground, be it much or little, without the special consent of the lord or his officers, and the whole jury and burgesses all jointly together. If such offences be committed it shall be lawful for certain of the jury to put it down again and lay it abroad, and the parties to be fined at the discretion of the jury then to be chosen."

Another use to which Collyhurst common was put was the practice of archery. In my second volume I referred to the law relating to the teaching and practice of archery, in connection with the butts that were erected in Garratt Lane. In 1560 the jury ordered that "the inhabitants within the town of Manchester shall make or cause to be made two pairs of butts;

that is to say that the inhabitants upon the south side of the church to make one pair of butts in the Manchester Lane; and the inhabitants on the north side of the church, one other pair of butts, upon Collyhurste." In the time of Queen Elizabeth, strong efforts were made by parliament to secure the continued practice of archery, which was gradually dying out.

The law laid it down that all boys above the age of seven years, and men should possess a bow and at least two shafts or arrows. Archery was to be practised by all on holy days, parents and employers being held responsible for seeing that their children and servants did so at least four times a year. The best bows were to be made of yew, but the bowyers for every bow they made of yew were to make four others "meet to shoot in, of elm, witch-hazel, ash or other wood proper for the same." The cheaper were to be used by the poorer classes who could not afford to pay from 6d. to 1s. the price of one made from yew. In closing these references to old Collyhurst common if may be noted that in an entry in the records for 1568 mention is made of a curious place name. A parcel of land called Tyll Hill had been granted to Ralph Pendleton and in making his boundary line he had exceeded his limits. He was therefore ordered to remove his fence to the proper line.

Collyhurst Common which had originally extended over eighty acres of land was as we have seen taken over by Rowland Mosley in 1605 with the exception of about six acres which was to be devoted to the accommodation of sufferers from the plague and to be used as a place of interment for those who died from the visitation. This land probably abutted on Collyhurst Clough which was at one time a delightfully wooded spot. As centuries passed the land appears to have been gradually enclosed and covered with buildings. Sixty years ago a small portion of it denuded of grass survived and was still known locally as the Common. When Rochdale Road was made in 1806 a number of human remains and a lead coffin were found in Collyhurst Clough reminiscences probably of the plague days referred to.

On the banks of the Irk that ran through the Clough on its journey from Blackley to Hunt's Bank on the site now occupied by St. James' Church stood Collyhurst Hall. The wooded dingle extended in front of the hall, and behind the house were spacious lawns and shrubberies which formed a remarkable contrast to that part of the city as we know it to-day. It was for several centuries a residence of a branch of the Mosley family. One of the last residents of Collyhurst Hall was Charles Ryder, a cotton manufacturer, whose warehouse was in Cannorn Street. Mr. Ryder was an active promoter of "Sunday Schools for children of all denominations," and was the founder of the one built in Elm Street, Oldham Road. He compiled a hymn-book, many copies of which he gave away to Sunday Schools and to persons interested in the Sunday School movement. He never married, and as his brother and two sisters died unmarried, the large property they owned passed to outsiders.

ROCHDALE ROAD.

Part II.

ABOUT SIXTY YEARS AGO.

A century ago a new road was made from Manchester to Middleton, and was known for many years as St. George's Road after the church of that name. As previously stated there had previously been a minor thoroughfare bearing the name of Back Lane, which gave access to Collyhurst. The present name of the road is Rochdale Road, although why the change should have been made from St. George's Road is not at all clear. The present widening of the thoroughfare has drawn more public notice to it than it has obtained for many years. Its condition and surroundings, so far as the city end of it is concerned, are far from being pleasant and desirable. The slums that bound it on both sides will cause many who pass along it to think that it is one of our oldest roads. Such is not the case, and much of the property to-day regarded as slums was, little more than half a century ago, fairly well situated.

In order to realise how much of the present state of things is of recent growth it is only necessary to pass along St. George's Road as it was about sixty years ago. As far as Coburg Street not only was the front land occupied, but the back land was filled up. The gas works stood at the bottom of Gould Street, and on the other side of the road were the premises of the railway company. St. George's Church, known when it was built as St. George's-in-the-Fields, was surrounded by open land. At Pilling Street the regularity of the buildings along the road ceased, and at intervals there were stretches of open land. One of these was almost opposite to the end of Pilling Street. Pilling Street and other streets on the left hand side of St. George's Road were short, and ended in fields across which could be seen the villa residences of Cheetham. The Roman Catholic Chapel and Nunnery in Livesey Street stood almost alone, the land from there to Osborne Street being unbuilt upon. Away across the fields on the opposite side of the main road was Vauxhall Gardens, a place of popular resort; and near by was a sandstone quarry. A little way past Osborne Street were the pits connected with the St. George's Colliery, and in the adjoining fields were several pits which formed an attraction for many of the lads of the neighbourhood. Brick-making was carried on on much of the land adjacent to the site of Collyhurst Old Hall. The Moston Brook was crossed by Collyhurst Bridge, the Clough extending for some distance on either side of the bridge. The water in the stream had lost some of its purity, but it was far from being the black stream that it must be to-day. A little distance before passing under Collyhurst Bridge it widened out very considerably, forming a reservoir. After passing over the Clough, the road was bounded on either side by a succession of fields, the first house in the direction of Harpurhey being Willow Cottage, that stood at the corner of Crampton's Lane, now represented by Queen's Road. On the opposite side of St. George's Road was the opening into a short narrow lane, which ended in a field path, which again opened out into Lamb Lane, in which there stood a few rural cottages together with two houses of greater dimensions, and known as Whitworth Hall and Collyhurst Lodge. A smithy stood at the corner of the lane referred to and St. George's Road; but only one house was passed on that side of the road until the cemetery on the opposite side of the road was reached. Hendham Hall, pleasantly situated, stood in its own grounds, which grounds were a few years later secured for the purposes of a public park, and as Queen's Park will be familiar to every reader. Harpurhey was nothing more than a small village consisting of about half a dozen lanes; the houses being about equally divided on the two sides of the road. Green Mount House and Green Mount Cottages stood surrounded by fields, and in the background in the opposite direction were the print works. Residence in Harpurhey in those days was a delightful experience. The air was pure, and from any part of the village open fields, not yet degraded into town crofts but smiling with verdure, could be seen. The smell of the new mown hay borne on the cool breeze of a summer's evening, and the sight of waving corn mellowing under a summer's sun were sights familiar to the resident of Harpurhey sixty years ago. Trade was represented by several widely separated buildings. At the bottom of Crampton's Lane, in Hendham Vale, was the brewery. A little distance away were the cotton and worsted dye works; whilst the neighbouring sandstone quarries found employment for a few men. Moston, embowered in trees, could be seen in the distance on the one hand, and on the other side St. Luke's Church stood out as a landmark. Such in brief is an account of Rochdale Road as it appeared to the visitor during the period familiarly known in another connection as the hungry forties. Roughly speaking, although the district on both sides of the thoroughfare were built up almost as far as Livesey Street, from there to just past Osborne Street a fringe of houses stood along the roadside with open crofts behind. But from there to Harpurhey the thoroughfare was a country road, bounded by fields with here and there a cottage, or, perhaps, a more pretensious residence standing in a garden, gay in summer time with sweet smelling flowers. Reference has been made to the making of the road in the early part of the last century. The Act of Parliament authorising the construction of the road was passed in 1797, but for some reason not explained little was done in the matter for several years and in 1802 a second Act was obtained, which bore the title "An Act for continuing the term, and altering and enlarging the powers of an Act passed in the thirty-eighth year of the reign of His present Majesty, entitled, 'An Act for more effectually repairing, widening, altering, and improving the road from the town of Manchester, by a place called the White Smithy, in the township of Crumpsall, to the town of Rochdale.'" The Act was further amended in 1813. The recent metamorphosis, the result of the introduction of the electric tramways system, needs no further reference.

Such developments were not anticipated when the

road was constructed a century ago. To the casual observer Rochdale Road, as it was a few years ago, formed a great contrast with either Oldham Road or Great Ancoats Street. The two last named are of sufficient width to meet all the requirements of probably another century's development and change. That width is to a certain extent owing to the fact that a century ago the houses that faced them had long gardens in front. The disappearance of the gardens and the substitution for them of wide footpaths accounts for some of the extra width of both thoroughfares. In the case of Rochdale Road, its formation having been a matter of comparatively recent history, the houses built upon it, at any rate at the city end, were built close up to the roadway without gardens.

ROCHDALE ROAD.

Part III.

TINKER'S OR VAUXHALL GARDENS.

To two generations of Manchester people Tinker's Gardens, or Vauxhall Gardens as they were latterly called, were a popular holiday resort; and to perhaps another generation they were a tradition, or little more than that. To-day there remains no trace of them, but occasionally as we come across one who in childhood's days was taken there, we may hear some account of their glories. To the present generation the institution is not even a name. It is therefore necessary to say something concerning this one-time popular resort. The ground once covered by the gardens is on the left hand side of Rochdale Road, some little distance away from that road, and lying between it and Collyhurst Road. The approach to them was near to the end of Osborne Street.

The proprietor for about forty years was Robert Tinker, who in Schole's Directory for 1797 as "Robert Tinker, Grape and Compass Coffee House and Tea Gardens, Collyhurst." In later years he became a victualler, and in 1814 he changed the name of his establishment to Vauxhall Gardens. For a fuller account of the glories of the gardens I must refer the reader to Alexander Wilson's *Johnny Green's Description of Tinker's Gardens* with which this chapter will be closed. On holidays and Sundays great crowds of people resorted to the gardens, where they could promenade or dance (except on Sundays) to the music of a brass band, and where they could partake of tea and other refreshments at small tables standing under overhanging trees or in alcoves covered with creepers. The situation of the gardens seems to have been very favourable to plant growth, and an announcement made in 1814 reads very curiously to-day. It ran thus:—"To the admirers of cucumbers. At these gardens may be seen a cucumber which measures seven feet eight inches long. One from the same plant was sent for the Prince Regent's inspection. It is allowed by all gardeners, and others who have seen it, to be the greatest curiosity of the kind Nature ever produced in this kingdom."

From time to time balloon ascents were made from the gardens, the last of these being made by Lieutenant Gale in 1847. Robert Turner died on February 1st, 1836, but the gardens were continued until about 1852 when their glories having departed they were closed. The subsoil consisted of a valuable bed of sand of a peculiar quality, used by iron moulders, and in the course of a few years the site was literally carted away. After the removal of the sand houses were built, and to-day the spot whereon Tinker's Gardens stood is indistinguishable in the maze of streets and rows of houses that now cover the district.

Mr. Procter in his volume *Manchester in Holiday Dress*, refers to an advertisement issued by Mr. Tinker in 1812, in which he announces special attractions to celebrate Wellington's great victory. The grounds were to be illuminated by means of three thousand variegated lamps which were to transform the gardens to an Elysian retreat. Popular vocalists were to supplement the efforts of the band, and the charge for admission was to be 1s. 6d. The entertainment, it was said, would render the evening "at once intellectual, rural, and delightful."

The following is Alexander Wilson's song, "Johnny Green's Description of Tinker's Gardens."

Heigh! Hall o' Nabs, an' Sam, an' Sue,
Why, Jonathan, art tew theere too?
We're aw aloike, there's nought to do,
  So bring us a quart before us.
Aw're at Tinker's gardens yesternoon,
An' whot aw seed, aw'll tell yo soon,
In a bran new song, boh it's to th' owd tune,
  Yo'st ha't if yo'll join meh chorus.

Aw geet some brass, fro' uncle Nat,
Eawr David lent mea his best hat,
Then off fur th' teawn aw seet full swat,
  Mich faster nor Pickfort's waggin.
Aw paid meh brass, an' in aw goes,
An' eh! what shady beawers i' rows,
Wheer lots o' ladies an' their beaus
  Wurn set to get their baggin.

There's bonfeoirs fix't at th' top o' pows,
To leet yor poipes, an' warm yor nose;
Then a thing to tell which way th' wind blows,
  An' th' fish pond too did pleas mea;
Boh th' reawnd-heawse is the rummest shop,
It's fix't on here an' there a prop,
Just loike a great umbrella top;
  If it's not, Jimmy Johnson squeeze mea.

Aw seed a cage as big, aw'll swear,
As a wild beast show i' Sawfort fair,
There's rappits, brids, an' somethings there,
  Aw couldna' gawm, by th' mass, mon;
Aw thowt o' pullink one chap's wigs,

For tellink me they're guinea pigs,
Says aw, 'Meh lad, aw'm up to yor rigs,
They're noan worth hawve o'th' brass, mon."

Aw met wi' a wench aw'd often seen,
When aw wi' meh wark to th' teawn had bin,
Hoo're drest as foine as ony queen,
So aw just stept up behind hur;
Says aw, 'Yung miss, dun yo wark for Kays?
Aw've wove their crankys scoores o' days,
Hoo wouldna' speak, boh walk'd hur ways,
An' hoo're nowt but a bobbin woinder.

Boh th' band o' music caps owd Nick,
Aw ne'er seed th' loikes sin aw wur wick;
Them drest loike soldiers, thrunk and thick,
As merry as hey-makers.
Up in a tree, foive yard fro' th' greawnd,
On a greyt big table, rail'd aw reawnd,
While lads an' wenches jigg'd to th' seawnd,
'Oh, merrily danced the Quakers.'

Then next aw seed a swing, by gad!
Where th' ladies flock'd loike hey-go-mad;
They wanted a roide far wor' than th' lads,
They really did, for sure.
Ther'n one wur drest so noice i' blue,
An' loike an' angel up hoo flew,
Hoo'd noice red cheeks, an' garters, too,
So aw thowt aw'd buck up to hur.

Aw made hur link wi' mich ado,
An' mounted up a greyt heigh brow
Wheer folk run up, an' deawn it too,
Just loike March hares, for sure.
So when eawr Kate coom we begun,
An' stearted off, twur glorious fun!
Mich faster than Cock Robin run,
When he won at Karsy Moor.

What wark we made, aw'm sheawmt to tell,
We tried, boh could no' stop eawrsel
Till into a beawer yed first aw fell,
Where aw th' foine folk wur set, mon.
Some porter run aw deawn my shirt;
A biscuit stuck to th' ladies skirt,
An whot wi' th' hurt, an' grease, an' dirt,
By gum, aw feel it yet, mon.

Of aw the things that pleast us, John,
Wur Tinker's house wi' pot dolls on;
There's Blucher an' Lord Wellington.
  An' Blue Beard look'd so glum, surs!
There's cupids under trees and shrubs,
An' men wi' harps, an' some wi' clubs,
An' naked childer up o' tubs,
  Don'd eawt i' lots o' plumbs, surs.

Reet hungry, aw seet mea deawn at last,
An' swallow'd cakes an' ale so fast,
Aw wonder meh waistcoat did no' brast,
  Aw'r full os meh hoide could crom, surs
When aw wur seen at could be seen,
They play'd, 'God save eawr noble Queen,'
Aw strid to th' tune reawnd th' bowling green,
  An' away aw coom streight whoam, surs.

It bangs booath play heawse, fair an' wakes,
For gam o' all maks, ale an' cakes,
Aw'll bet a quart, an' theaw'st howd th' stakes,
  It bangs th' king's creawnation.
Aw'd ha' yo't goo next Monday noon,
For if't rains poikels, late or soon,
Aw'll goo again, if aw goo bowt shoon,
  For it's th' grandest place i' th' nation."

And such was the opinion of many of the folk who lived in Manchester and the district seventy years ago.

ROCHDALE ROAD.

PART IV.

ST. GEORGE'S FIELDS AND CHURCH.

St. George's Church, which gave the name by which the fields surrounding it were known for many years, was built in the closing decade of the nineteenth century. There seems to be a good deal of mystery with reference to its origin and early history. When it was built Back Lane was a narrow, country lane, and Newton Lane, as Oldham Road was then called, was a fine, wide country road bounded by fields with, at intervals, a few cottages. The site of the present railway premises were almost entirely unbuilt upon, although a small amount of building had taken place in the vicinity of the Shude Hill pits. But after making all due allowances, there does not appear to have been an adequate reason for building a church in what was almost an isolated position. This would account for the statement made concerning the church by Aston in his *Manchester Guide*. He says: "St. George's Church is a large brick building with a tower of the same materials, in which is a small bell, situated near Newton Lane. It is in the same predicament as Saint Clement's with respect to consecration, and has been in the hands of several ministers. Report says it was built as a speculation for profit, but that it has been, what all religious speculations should be, a losing concern. It was opened for public worship, after having been shut up half finished for several years, on Sunday, April 1st, 1798. The pulpit is mahogany, and there is a small organ in the church. It has a burial place which has not yet been enclosed. The present minister is the Rev. Mr. Johnson." Such was the account given in Aston's *Manchester Guide*, published in 1804. In a later edition, undated, but published in 1826, he gives the additional items of information that "The last dissenting minister was the Rev. Robert Bradley, who was subsequently ordained by the Bishop, and is now Chaplain to the Manchester Workhouse. The church was purchased by subscription, and consecrated January 17th, 1818." The Rev. W. Johnson died in 1828, and was succeeded by the Rev. James White, M.A., who was born at Nottingham, in 1788, and was the younger brother of Kirke White, the poet. He remained in Manchester until 1841, taking an active interest in the promotion of Sunday Schools and infant schools. In 1831 he founded the Manchester Clerical Book Club. He died at Sloley House, Scotton, Norfolk, in March, 1885. It is recorded as a proof of the confidence and respect in which he was held whilst incumbent of St. George's that Mr. White was allowed to appoint two wardens to the parishioners one, a custom which continued under the regime of his successor.

As time progressed the Lancashire and Yorkshire Railway Company found it necessary to extend their premises at Oldham Road, and the fate of the church was sealed. The building was pulled down and the congregation removed to a new church bearing the same name in Oldham Road. The new church, towards the erection of which Mr. C. J. Heywood gave £10,000, was consecrated by Bishop Fraser in 1877. The fields that surrounded the church for many years after its erection, were from time to time the scene of great gatherings of poor men either advocating reform or protesting against injustice.

One of these took place about a century ago—in 1809. Wages in all branches of trade were low, and they were perhaps as low amongst the weavers as in any other trade. An agitation for an increase in the weavers' pay was commenced, and a meeting was held on St. George's Fields. Amongst the leading townsmen of those days Colonel Hanson occupied a high position. He had strong sympathies for the workers, and it is said he had a silver shuttle appended to each side of his carriage. When the meeting was being addressed by Mr. Hanson a party of opponents approached and for some time matters wore a very threatening aspect. Supported by cavalry and infantry was the borough-reeve along with the magistrates, special constables, the runners and Joseph Nadin. The riot act was read, and Mr. Hanson speaking on horseback urged the people to disperse peaceably. This they were doing when the crowd was alarmed at seeing the horses of the dragoons approaching. In a moment there was disorder and panic; and matters were not improved by certain of the dragoons discharging their weapons, as a result of which a man, an onlooker standing at his own door, was shot. This was ten years before Peterloo. The period around 1826 was marked by distress in a very aggravated form, and despairing of obtaining justice or even a fair hearing of their case, the more desperate of the leaders of the workers had recourse to damage to property. In the outside districts around Manchester factories were attacked, and the machinery destroyed. In the town itself nothing of this nature had taken place, the agitators contenting themselves with placing before public meetings statements of their grievances. On April 27th a body of men marched through the streets of the town, announcing that a meeting of the unemployed would be held on St. George's Fields in the evening. The meeting commenced at six o'clock and the first speaker urged his hearers to commence an attack upon the factories in order to destroy the looms they contained. Others followed in the same strain, until a later speaker advocated another policy. He announced that at a meeting held in the town that morning £1000 had been subscribed to meet the distress, that the King had sent £1000 for the same object, that next day 20,000 lbs. of bacon and 100,000 lbs. of meal would be ready for free distribution, and that the workers would be more likely to advance their cause by working for the repeal of the corn laws and other necessary reforms. These counsels very largely prevailed, and although Beaver's factory in Jersey Street was burnt down the same night, little damage to property accompanied the agitation of 1826.

Three years later another period of distress and suffering overtook the workers in the cotton manufacturing districts. The proceedings of a number of persons who assembled on St. George's Fields on May 3rd, 1829 may be recounted as showing the state of affairs in Lancashire at that time. Having met as arranged, the crowd prcceeded to Mr. Guest's factory in Union Street, and prevailed upon his weavers to leave their looms. From there they proceeded to a factory in Mather Street where, after persuading the weavers to leave their work, they demolished the whole of the looms, etc. After this they tossed the cloth in the building into the streets where it was either trampled under foot or stolen. At Harbottle's factory in Pollard Street they destroyed forty-six power looms, smashed scores of windows, and did other damage. They then returned to Mr. Guest's factory, where they destroyed fifty-three looms, and threw a quantity of cloth into the canal. At this juncture the police appeared, but only being few in numbers they retreated before a pursuing mob. They took refuge in the Albion Hotel where some of the magistrates were sitting. The crowd returning to St. George's Road burst open the doors of Parker's factory in Ludgate Street and set fire to it. The building was a large one, being forty yards long, twenty wide; and seven stories high. So intense was the blaze that cottages on three sides of the mill took fire and a general conflagration seemed to be imminent when the appearance of the military caused the mob to retreat. Such were some of the scenes that marked the history of St. George's Fields.

As we have previously seen, the road known as St. George's Road is now known as Rochdale Road, and the Church dedicated to St. George, and known as St. George's-in-the-Fields, has disappeared ; and now it remains to be said that for more than half a century St. George's Fields have been represented by a much extended goods station and long rows of houses facing into narrow streets and forming a portion of one of the most densely populated districts in the city, St. Michael's Ward.

ROCHDALE ROAD.

PART V.

REV. W. GADSBY AND HIS CHAPEL.

When Aston issued his *Manchester Guide* a little more than a century ago the members of the Baptist persuasion in Manchester met for worship in two chapels. One of these was the old building referred to in a previous chapter, and known as the Coldhouse Chapel, and one in Back Lane, afterwards known as Rochdale Road. The latter had been built in 1789, and stood for many years in the midst of fields. The story of the building was quite uneventful until 1803 when the Rev. William Gadsby came as "supply" until a permanent appointment could be made. His earnestness and originality produced such an impression upon the congregation that he was appointed pastor in 1805, a position that he held until his death thirty-nine years later.

The Rev. William Gadsby occupied so prominent a position in the religious life of the city for many years, that although not by birth a Manchester man, his career at Rochdale Road demands a somewhat lengthy notice. He was born of very humble parents at Attleborough, in the parish of Nuneaton, in 1773, and received only a very scanty education. He said of his education: "As for what the world calls learning, I have but little of it. It was not in my parent's power

Rev. William Gadsby.

to put me to school to learn to write, much less to learn grammar; and though I was taught a little to read, yet in those days of youth and folly, I in a great measure forgot it, so that when I was called by Divine Grace I was not able to read tolerably well one chapter in the Bible." He worked at ribbon weaving until he was twenty-two years old, when, owing to chest weakness he was compelled to give up the trade, and adopt that of stocking weaving. When twenty years of age he was baptised by Mr. Aston in Cow Lane, Coventry. Mr. Aston said of him then that he could see something in the young man, "although so illiterate and uncouth, that seemed blessedly to prove that he would some day or other be made very useful to God's dear family." In 1796 he married Elizabeth Marvin, Six years before marriage he had been converted to a contemplation of religious matters by seeing a triple execution at Coventry. He attended prayer meetings and endeavoured to follow a godly life, but it was not until after his marriage that his mind became exercised about the work of the ministry. "Preach," he used to say, "he would not, and yet the Lord having firmly laid hold on him he could get no rest." He prayed that he might die rather than be sent to preach, and one night actually got out of bed and sat on the cellar steps so that he might take cold and die. "But," he said, "I could not take cold for the life of me." After resisting the promptings of his conscience for some time he surrendered and began preaching. His own words describing the decision are characteristic and quaint. "Well, Lord, if this is the way Thou workest, Thou never hadst a bigger fool to deal with."

His first sermon was preached on Whit Monday, 1798 from 1 Peter, ii. 7, "Unto you therefore which believe, He is precious." He used to say in connection with this sermon that in order to introduce his text he began with reading the first chapter of the Epistle, but if he might have had the world he could not have read the hard names contained in the first and second verses, but just slurred them over.

His first appointment had been to a small chapel at Desford, where he commenced preaching in 1800 and remained there until he was selected to fill the pulpit at St. George's Road. As a preacher he belonged to the class once very common in Lancashire and Yorkshire. Plain in speech, with a deep rich vein of humour which he could not or would not attempt to suppress in his preaching, he drew large congregations. Many of his anecdotes were extremely droll; and his similes were of the homeliest description. His peculiarities often drew upon him the adverse criticism of some of the more precise members of other congregations; and one old Baptist called upon him one day and reasoned with him seriously about being so peculiar. Gadsby telling of the visit said: "He told me that if only I would be a little more calm, modify my sentiments a little, and not be quite so savage, the other ministers would take me by the hand: and I said to myself after he was gone: Well, after all, why should I be so singular? I certainly should have more peace and more honour, too; and so I made up my mind to be more moderate. Accordingly on the following Lord's Day I began to preach in a way that would offend no one as I thought. I screwed my mouth like a corkscrew, and was determined I would be very mild. But, Oh! what bondage I felt, till this passage came to my mind with great power, 'He that hath My word, let him speak My words faithfully.' In the name of the Lord it must come out. I stamped with my foot and thumped with my fist, and I never preached more savagely in my life, and from that day to this the devil never got me into that box again." He always insisted that if the truth took possession of a man's heart it would influence his life in general, and make him more generous. Preaching on one occasion for a friend in whose congregation there was a merchant worth many thousands of pounds, and who, although he was always saying how much he profited by the sermons he heard, never gave a farthing more to the Church funds than his seat rent of six shillings a year. After the service the man went into the vestry and told Gadsby the customary tale. "I don't believe you," said the preacher. The man seemed surprised, but assured him that it was quite true. "Then," replied Gadsby, "the Bible can't be true, for it says: 'By their fruits ye shall know them,' and if all your fruit is one and sixpence a quarter the root cannot be worth much." As a Baptist he preached adult immersion, and on one occasion drove his teaching home in a characteristic fashion. "If," he said, "sprinkling be sufficient, what was the use of Philip taking the eunuch to a place where there was much water? Bless my heart, with a bucket of water and a besom I could sprinkle the whole of this congregation." On another occasion he spoke in a sermon on the request of the mother of Zebedee's children: "Lord, let my sons sit one on Thy right hand and the other on Thy left when Thou comest to thy kingdom." "Woman, thou knowest not what thou askest." "I should think hoo didn't," said Gadsby; and then he said, "What two nice young men those must have been. They darn't ask themselves, so they sent their mother."

In 1836 a musical festival was held in Manchester for the benefit of the charities. In the morning sacred music was to be performed in the "Old Church," and in the evening a fancy dress ball was to be held in the theatre, at which some of the clergymen were to be present in their gowns. Gadsby preached a sermon against this, what he called "awful profanity." "A report was circulated that the Church and the Theatre had been courting a long time, and that they were to be married the following week." Speaking on the occasion of the death of an active member of his congregation, he eulogised her character and work, but ended with the words: "Now you'll think hoo was an angel. You were never more mistaken in your life. Hoo were sometimes as nazzy an owd piece as I ever knew in my life." He sometimes introduced phrases into his prayers worded in the same homely fashion, as, for instance, when referring to the government of the day, he said: "Thou knowest, O Lord, that many of Thy servants before Thee have houses, and to those houses are attached gardens in which they grow peas, potatoes, cabbages, and other vegetables for the use of their families; and Thou knowest also that the neighbour's pigs are apt to stray into these gardens, and do incalculable mischief by uprooting and devouring the produce, to prevent which they have a habit of ringing their noses; and do Thou, O Lord, in Thy infinite mercy, so ring the noses of His Majesty's ministers that they, in like manner, may be prevented from uprooting our glorious constitution."

Archibald Prentice, in the *Manchester Times*, wrote "A Memoir of Gadsby would be highly interesting to the student of mental philosophy. It would afford a striking contradiction to the doctrine of the Owenites that man is a creature of circumstances; for he rose triumphant by the strength of natural genius, directed by right religious principles, from circumstances which might have influenced the life and conduct of one of inferior intellect, but which he brushed aside as the elephant displaces the canes in a jungle. In any station he would have been a remarkable man, just as Burns would have been remarkable had he never written a line of poetry."

In appearance Mr. Gadsby was rather below middle height, and in his old age had a clear and a ruddy complexion, with a round pleasant face. He also at this time wore a black velvet skull cap in the pulpit. It has been denied that he ever preached in his shirt sleeves, but this is not correct, for one who had often heard him preach told Mr. J. C. Lockhart that he had heard him preach so attired. On each occasion it happened to be an exceedingly hot day, and he deliberately took off his coat and placed it over the side of the pulpit before he began to preach. He was an indefatigable worker for, in addition to conducting three or four services weekly in his own chapel, he would often preach four or five sermons elsewhere.

Many times the following would be his programme. After preaching three times at home on the Sunday he would walk on the Monday morning to Rochdale, where he would have dinner. In the afternoon, after another four-mile walk, he would reach a chapel where he would preach, afterwards returning to Rochdale, where he would preach in the evening. Walking home on Tuesday, he would conduct service at St. George's Road the same evening, and on Thursday walk to Bolton, preaching in the evening and returning home on Friday. He calculated that in the course of thirty-six years he travelled on foot no less a distance than sixty thousand miles, and opened forty chapels in Yorkshire, Lancashire, Derbyshire and Cheshire.

Mr. Slugg, in his *Reminiscences of Manchester Fifty Years Ago*, says of Gadsby, who by the way strongly objected to the designation of Reverend, "I remember something of his appearance, which was not clerical according to the notions of the present day. He was rather over the average height, wore knee breeches —frequently both they and his stockings being coloured —and an unstiffened white handkerchief tied in a bow. His face had a somewhat quaint and humorous expression, and his countenance was rather florid. The valley of Rossendale fifty years ago contained several Baptist chapels, and when my father lived at Bacup, Mr. Gadsby frequently preached in one or other of the chapels. On these occasions he used to let fly his envenomed arrows at the Arminian doctrines of Methodism, which are so much opposed to the Calvinism he preached. I do not care to repeat the sayings which it was currently reported he had uttered, some of them both coarse and bitter beyond belief. Every Tuesday evening he preached in his own chapel, when the congregation consisted generally of the members of his church. On these occasions he laid aside all controversy and the style which he adopted sometimes when in the presence of a mixed congregation, and talked to his flock as a father to his family. The only time of my hearing him was on such an occasion, when his discourse was a beautiful and experimental exposition of divine truth." He died in 1844 at the age of 71. The old chapel in which he preached has now been replaced by a more modern edifice, but the memory of the eccentric but much beloved pastor of the first half of the last century still remains a treasured possession of the members of the congregation assembling there.

ROCHDALE ROAD.

Part VI.

THE PUBLIC PARKS MOVEMENT.

Prior to 1844 Manchester had no public parks, nor recreation grounds. In the early days of the century, when most houses had gardens connected with them, and when the open fields extended down almost to the Collegiate Church, the question of open spaces for purposes of recreation had never been raised. One reason for this was the fact that the community had not been educated in the question. The majority of people belonged to the working classes, who under ordinary conditions had very little time for purposes of recreation. The hours of labour were long, and holidays were scarce. On Sundays they could walk to one of the many tea gardens that were to be found in the outskirts of the town; at Whit Week they could attend the races on Kersal Moor, and at Easter the glories of Knott Mill fair were provided for them. Beyond these limits and the attractions of the bar parlour there was nothing in the way of recreation provided for the workers of the population. So far as the children were concerned they could play in the streets, but seeing that they were usually drafted off to some kind of work as early as eight or nine years of age, they had little need for playgrounds. The wealthier portion of the community regarded their poorer neighbours as beasts of toil, and probably if the suggestion had been made that they should be provided with parks and recreation grounds it would have been regarded with feelings akin to horror as savouring of revolution. The passing of the Reform Bill of 1832, the gradual growth of education, and the general advance of reform movements brought about a great change in the generally accepted views on a variety of subjects, one of which was the necessity for the provision of public parks and recreation grounds.

When the question was first seriously discussed in Manchester, now more than sixty years ago, the town, although growing in all directions, was very different from the city of to-day. In almost every direction open country could be found within a radius of about a mile from Piccadilly, and in many cases uncovered fields were to be found much nearer than that distance.

Early in 1844 the question of providing parks was very much debated, and in June of that year a requisition was framed and signed by over one hundred and ten firms and private individuals, and was presented to the Mayor, Alexander Kay. As a result a public meeting was held on August 8th in the Town Hall "to consider the propriety of taking steps for the formation of a public park, walk or playground." A subscription list was opened, and in a few weeks over £8000 had been raised. Lord Francis Egerton, Sir Benjamin Heywood, and Mark Philips each subscribed £1000, and six other gentlemen gave £500 each. Great enthusiasm was evinced in the project, and workmen's committees were formed, who collected small amounts from the working people. These committees in all collected over £2,000, a fine contribution from the workers themselves. In all £35,000 was obtained, a sum sufficiently large to enable the "Committee for the Formation of Public Parks in Manchester" to purchase three estates. The first one secured was the Lark Hill estate, the residence of Mr. William Garnett, for which £5,000 was paid, of which £500 was returned by Mr. Garnett as his subscription to the movement. To the Lark Hill estate the adjacent land known as Walness Flat was added, and the whole, comprising over thirty-eight acres, was laid out and named Peel Park. The second estate to be secured was the Hendham Hall estate, over thirty acres in extent, the property of Jonathan Andrew, for which the sum of £7250 was paid. When completed it was named Queen's Park. The third purchase was that of thirty-one acres of land, a portion of the Bradford estate, from Lady Houghton for £6200. In honour of Mark Philips this park was named after him. The purchases were all made in the spring of 1845, and for more than a year they were in the gardeners' and workmen's hands. The opening of the three parks took place on August 22nd, 1846, the occasion being marked by great processions and rejoicings.

Since 1846 the number of our parks has been increased to fifteen, in addition to which there are about forty open spaces owned by the Corporation and used as recreation grounds. In 1846 the three parks serving Manchester and Salford covered about one hundred acres of land. To-day Manchester's parks cover an area of nearly a thousand acres, to which must be added the Salford parks covering nearly 120 acres. The Manchester recreation grounds cover 146 acres, and those of Salford about 88. The hundred acres of 1846 is therefore represented to-day by 1354 acres; and although the acreage is small as compared with that of a few cities, it shows a splendid development of a system inaugurated only sixty years since.

BEFORE THE FORMATION OF QUEEN'S PARK.

Jonathan Andrew, from whom the committee referred to purchased Hendham Hall, was a successful merchant who had resided there for about a quarter of a century. When Mr. Andrew took up his residence at the Hall, Harpurhey was only a very small place. Before dealing with that a few words might be said with reference to the origin and meaning of the place name Harpurhey, of which Hendham Park formed a portion. Harland derives the name from Hearpere, the Anglo Saxon for a male harper, and Hey, meaning a field. On the other hand we read that in 1322 William Harpour held eighty acres of land on lease for life from John de la Warre. It is curious that the eighty acres referred to would equal about 160 statute acres, and that the acreage of Harpurhey is returned at 163 statute acres.

Let us now glance at Harpurhey at the time that Mr. Andrew took up his residence at Hendham Hall. Aston, in his *Lancashire Gazetteer*, says of the hamlet, "This small township has many pleasant situations in it and commands some views of Blakeley Valley, Smedley, and of Heaton House, which are picturesquely beautiful. The township in 1821 contained fifty-nine houses, occupied by fifty-six families, five of which were employed in agriculture, and fifty in manufactures of various kinds. The population was 297, of which 148 were males and 149 females. The place was of such small importance in those days that the directory contains not more than a dozen entries relative to it. Five of these have reference to members of the Andrew family. Edward Andrew, gentleman, resided at Harpurhey Cottage. Andrew and Tarlton carried on business as turkey-red and fancy dyers at the works that stood on the banks of the river Irk, near to the quarries. Robert Andrew lived at Green Mount and Gilbert Tarlton at Irkton Cottage. Thomas Andrew owned the print works also on the banks of the Irk, and resided at Harpurhey; and, finally, Jonathan Andrew occupied Hendham Hall. He was a merchant whose warehouse was 42 Church Street in 1824 and afterwards at 65 High Street. Before taking up his residence at Harpurhey he lived at his place of business then at 11 George Street.

Mention has been made of Crampton's Lane. When Mr. Andrew removed to Hendham Hall it was a quiet country lane, bounded on both sides by fields. About two hundred yards from the highway the lane turned sharp to the right leading to the brewery and the other works standing thereabouts on the bank of the river. At the bend referred to stood the Collyhurst Paper Mill. When Queen's Road was constructed the lane was continued beyond this point until Smedley Road was reached, and was then continued along Job's Stile Lane. Behind the hall, alongside the river, was Hendham Vale, the banks of which in one place was blue in early summer with the bluebells as the wild narcissus is commonly called, which grew there in profusion. Near by daffodils could be gathered and in the meadows could be found the pale primrose. The country round the park had not lost its charm, and the conditions of life were well nigh as primitive as obtains to-day only in very remote country districts. This was when Mr. Andrew took up his residence at Harpurhey, and when, more than twenty years later he sold the park the district had lost little of its charm. Certainly the village had extended a little; a few more houses had been built, but the air was still pure and the summer's sky was still unclouded by factory smoke. A second village inn had been licensed, but the Golden Lion still remained the popular house of call. The original building was black and white, but that in course of time was replaced by a more modern structure.

A MEETING OF BOTANISTS.

Mr. Grindon mentions a great gathering of botanists that met at the Golden Lion in August 1858. The house was the meeting place of a local botanical society and was the scene of many interesting gatherings. Botany as a study could then be followed within a few miles from the centre of the city. The Harpurhey botanists found abundance of matters to interest them in the cloughs through which the Irk flowed, and in the adjacent fields. On the special occasion referred to, just half a century ago, nearly thirty botanical societies foregathered at the Golden Lion. Some 212 persons attended, all of whom with the exception of about half a dozen, were working men. Many of the best known Lancashire botanists were there and a fine collection of specimens was brought together. James Percival junior took the chair and he showed his capabilities as a botanical student by naming some 150 of the specimens on view, giving first their Latin and then their English names, with brief notes on their nature or habits. When he had finished his task John Nowell named a collection of mosses, and T. Stansfield did the same with a large number of ferns. The three performances were particularly notable and the whole forms a record not likely to be equalled again in Manchester annals.

Leaving the Golden Lion with its associations we may close the present chapter with a brief note on the Harpurhey Cemetery. It was opened in September, 1837, but was not used very much for a few years. During the seventy years it has existed it has been selected as the last resting place of many well-known Manchester citizens. Amongst the more recent interments was that of John Owens, the "Old Mortality" of our city, whose collection of manuscripts forms a very interesting and valuable section of the books to be found at the Reference Library, King Street. In this long range of volumes is recorded the proceeds of a life's research into the past history of our city and other districts. He spent the whole of his life in or near to the city, and his remains now repose near those of another Manchester worthy, Ben Brierley, Amongst those who have occupied the post of registrar is included that of John Bolton Rogerson, one of the leading spirits in the gatherings that made Poet's Corner famous

Harpurhey Cemetery in 1843.

ROCHDALE ROAD.

PART VII.

A ROMAN CATHOLIC CHAPEL AND A NOTABLE PRIEST.

In 1832 the Roman Catholics opened a Roman Catholic Chapel, which had been erected on a piece of land lying between St. George's Road and Oldham Road, and approached by a street now known as Livesey Street. In those days the population that had collected at the city end of St. George's Road was very largely Irish, and it was probably in recognition of that fact that the new place of worship was dedicated to Ireland's patron saint, St. Patrick. Its first ministers were the Rev. D. Hearne, the Rev. J. Smith and the Rev. J. Hearne.

Of the many priests who have been associated with the Roman Catholic Chapels of Manchester none have done better work than Father Daniel Hearne, none have been imbued with broader feelings of toleration, and none have been more beloved by the members of their congregations. When St. Patrick's was built there was a strong feeling amongst the Roman Catholic population in favour of the appointment of the Rev. Peter Kaye, of St. Chad's, to the new chapel, but the Bishop of what was then called "the Northern District" appointed Father Hearne.

One who remembered him well described him in

the following terms: "He was an Irish priest who was exceedingly popular with his Manchester countrymen, a man who could and did dilate with genuine eloquence on the wrongs of Ireland, and who also bore a wonderful resemblance—a resemblance perfectly startling in countenance and physique—to the then living political and parliamentary force, Daniel O'Connell. Shortly after the Bishop's decision had taken effect the Rev. Peter Kaye, speaking at a meeting in St. Patrick's district, remarked in his jocular way that he so loved the Irish that his might almost be the motto of the Fitzgeralds, *i.e.*, "More Irish than the Irish themselves."

At the time that Father Hearne lived in Livesey Street a Wesleyan minister, the Rev. John Smith, resided there also; and these two men, holding very different views on matters theological, agreed to drop their differences when dealing with social questions; and they set a noble example by uniting themselves together in the work of Christian charity by house-to-house visitation and the distribution of relief without distinction of sect or creed. Mr. Joseph Johnson tells two striking stories of Father Hearne, which go to show with what love he was regarded by the poor brethren who formed by far the greater portion of his flock. One is well worth repeating.

"Father Hearne, by the way, was a character. He was very fond of youngsters, and from some cause I became a special favourite of his. One day, walking with him up Rochdale Road, my hand in his, a great crowd completely blocked the street. A fight was going on, a ring being kept, as we could see, by a number of brush-stales appearing above the heads of the crowd. The good Father quickly placed me in a doorway, telling me not to move until he returned, and then sprang into the crowd, wielding a mahogany stick, which he let fall upon the shoulders of all indiscriminately. A thunderbolt could not have cleared the street quicker or more completely; no one attempted to retaliate. Notwithstanding this rough method of reproving the members of his church, he was greatly beloved; by the poor he was almost worshipped."

Within three months from the date of the opening of the chapel the town was visited by one of the most terrible scourges that the inhabitants have suffered from since the days of the plague. Asiatic Cholera had appeared at Liverpool, and on May 17th, 1832 a man named James Palfreyman, living in Somerset Street, Dalefield, was seized with symptoms, which medical men pronounced to be that of malignant cholera. The disease spread with alarming rapidity through the most thickly populated areas of the town, and in August it reached its height. In that month there were 650 fresh cases reported in Manchester alone. In all, from May to December there were in Manchester, Salford and Chorlton-on-Medlock, 2113 cases, of which 920 resulted fatally. For the treatment of many cases, when home treatment was impossible, a special hospital was erected in Swan Street. The members of the medical profession rendered splendid services to the poor victims, but in some way or other the prejudices of the people were strongly aroused against them, and on September

3rd an attack was made on the hospital. Nine patients were removed, and had it not been that the crowd were prevented, it was believed that the whole of the inmates would have been removed, and that the building would have been set on fire. In the building was found a coffin containing the body of a boy who had died and whose head had been severed from the body, probably in the course of a post mortem examination. The head was held up by the ring-leaders of the disturbance, and served still further to exasperate the mob. During the whole of those terrible months no one in the town was more assiduous in his endeavours to relieve the sufferings of the victims of the disease; and to alleviate the distress and terror that equally possessed most of the survivors in the Rochdale Road district, than was Father Hearne. He was to many a sufferer a ministering angel, and it mattered not to him whether the unfortunate ones were members of his own Church or not, for in all cases his services were cheerfully rendered.

Leaving these records of suffering let us now turn to another incident in Father Hearne's career at St. Patrick's. In 1843 a new organ was built in the church, and was opened by Henry Smart, the great organist, of London. Mass was celebrated by the Honourable and Rev. George Spencer, brother of Lord Spencer, and the sermon was preached by Father Theobald Mathew, the great temperance reformer, who came in response to an urgent invitation from Father Hearne. After the service the great temperance advocate preached from the steps of a large stone cross in the graveyard. After preaching he administered to the kneeling crowd the pledge to abstain from all intoxicants. Hundreds took the pledge, and amongst the earliest to do so were two Unitarian ministers, the Rev. P. P. Carpenter, of Stand, and the Rev. F. Howarth, of Bury. Night and night saw a repetition of the scene, thousands of persons belonging to all denominations attending the services, which were held in the open air when the weather permitted. On Friday, July 21st, a tea party attended by three thousand persons, and presided over by Mr. James Kershaw, afterwards M.P. for Stockport, was held in the Free Trade Hall; and on the following day a great demonstration was held in Stevenson Square, at which the members of the Manchester and Salford Protestant Temperance Society and other temperance organisations supported the great preacher. It was estimated that at the meetings held in connection with the week's mission no fewer than seventeen thousand persons signed the pledge, each of them receiving an enrolment card and a medal.

In June, 1846, Father Hearne removed to London, to the great disappointment of many members of his Manchester congregation. To show the respect in which he was held and the appreciation for his many services a public meeting was held on June 15th in the Free Trade Hall, in his honour. A testimonial was presented to him consisting of a green silk purse containing two hundred and seventy pounds in gold, a large and splendid gold crucifix and chain valued at £40, a gold watch and chain, and a silver breakfast service.

Since the change that has come over the district

during the last sixty years commenced, many other places of worship have been opened, and have pursued the " even tenour of their way." These include Christ Church, Harpurhey, and the Albert Memorial Church in Queen's Road. The latter, which cost £4,400 to build, was consecrated on April 25th, 1864, was built in honour of the Prince Consort who had died about three years before.

In Harpurhey the first dissenting body to build a place of worship were the Wesleyan Methodists, whose chapel was opened in 1828, after services had been held for some time in private houses. The remaining places of worship—not so numerous as in some other parts of the city—are of comparatively recent origin; and although the various churches have done much to improve the conditions of life in the Rochdale Road district, an abundance of work still remains to be done.

ROCHDALE ROAD.

PART VIII.

THE ROAD IN 1839.

I have, in an earlier chapter, sketched the general appearance of the road as it was about seventy years ago. Let us now note a few other features that were familiar to the residents of 1839. In the first place the name of St. George's Road was still applied to the part of the thoroughfare that extended from Shudehill to Nelson Street, where it became Rochdale Road. The last houses in Rochdale Road were just past Buckley Street, and were numbered 287 and 289. This was, of course, on the left hand side. On the opposite side there were only about half a dozen houses in the Rochdale Road section of the thoroughfare Beyond these limits on both sides were open fields, which extended to the confines of Collyhurst, which was thus isolated from the town. It is noteworthy that in the half mile of roadway referred to there were no fewer than eight fully licensed houses in addition to eleven beerhouses. Although much of the back land at the Shudehill end of the road had been covered with houses and the population was steadily increasing, the number of licensed houses seems to have been unreasonably high. Another comparison may be made. Although there were eighteen licensed houses there were only eight bakers' shops, eight grocers, and six boot and shoe dealers. There was one bookseller, L. Coffey, who carried on business at number 100; and at 156 music was represented by W. R. Shaw, who kept a music shop and tuned pianos. It would seem that the residents were somewhat extravagant in the matter of their personal appearance, for the list of residents includes the names of half a dozen hair dressers. Beyond these brief notes the residents of the Rochdale Road of the late thirties do not seem to merit notice. To a small extent they were probably representative of a somewhat better type of tenant than we find there to-day; but as a rule they would belong to the same class.

We will therefore pass on to Collyhurst, which comprised the length of Rochdale Road extending from near to Osborne Street to Crampton's Lane, and Collyhurst Road from just beyond Dalton Street to the junction with Rochdale Road. Taking Rochdale Road first, there were just beyond Osborne Street the St. George's Collieries, which were owned by Edmund Buckley, who was M.P. for Newcastle-under-Lyme from 1841 to 1847, received the honour of baronetcy in 1868, resided for many years at Higher Ardwick, and was a prominent member of the John Shaw and Scramble Clubs. An account of Sir Edmund appeared in my second volume. A little distance beyond the collieries was the Collyhurst Clough Chemical Works; and adjacent to the bridge that crosses the Moston Brook was a logwood mill worked by John Appleton. Mr. Appleton's house, pleasantly situated in the Clough. stood apart from any others, the nearest being one attached to Ellam's ropewalk. From there to Crampton's

Lane the open fields were continued; the only houses being a few that stood some distance away from the road and known as White House Cottages. These were the only features that would be noticed in walking from Osborne Street to the site of Queen's Road seventy years ago.

Collyhurst Road was a little more interesting, and was certainly more picturesque, although the pedestrian passing that way to-day will hardly be able to realise that it at any time merited such a description. In the first place, just as the road was entered upon from Portland Street a number of pleasant gardens stood on the left hand side opposite to the end of Dalton Street. Near to the gardens was the Travis Isle Corn Mill; and a little distance away was the Collyhurst Dye Works, worked by Henry Worthington. Passing by Tinker's Gardens, which lay off the right hand side of the road, a red sandstone quarry and another logwood mill was passed. Along the banks of the river Tib were other dye works known variously as the Little Green, the Yew Tree, and the Cheetham Vale Dye Works. Perhaps the prettiest part of the road was that near to where Smedley Road joined it. Not only were the buildings very few in number, but an abundance of trees gave an additional charm to the spot. The isolated houses were all surrounded by gardens, and a few yards away on the left the River Tib ran through the fields. Just before reaching the junction of the road with Rochdale Road away across the fields would be seen the paper mills owned by and worked for several generations by a family of the name of Crampton. The population of the district was only small, the number of entries in the directory under the heading of Collyhurst being under a score. Included amongst these was Joseph Zanetti, who was partner in the firm of Agnew and Zanetti, and whose father, Vittore, founded the concern now so well known as Thomas Agnew and Sons. None of the other residents achieved more than a very local and flitting fame, the greater part being connected with one or other of the small works that have been referred to.

Seventy years ago Harpurhey village was about a quarter of a mile in length, the greater number of the houses facing the Rochdale Road, although after passing Crampton's Lane few were to be seen until the entrance to the cemetery was passed. Persons now living remember that when you walked from Osborne Street to the cemetery you would not pass more than about a dozen houses. These included Green Mount Place, where Benjamin Binyon, the tea dealer of Market Street, lived. Next door but one to him lived the Rev. James White, incumbent of St. George's-in-the-Fields.

The village of those days extended from the cemetery to the Post Office, which stood near to Harpurhey Cottage, and between these limits the road was built up on both sides, in addition to which a number of side streets had been formed. The place name of Green Mount seems to have been popular, for in addition to the Green Mount Place just mentioned, there was Green Mount House, a mansion standing in fairly extensive grounds, Green Mount Cottage, and Green Mount, the residence of Joseph Leese, a founder of the well-known firm of Kershaw, Leese and Sidebottom.

Another resident at that time was William C. Chew, the founder of the firm of solicitors of that name. His place of business was at 23 Swan Street. Several members of the Andrew family, in addition to Jonathan Andrew of Hendham Hall, were still resident in the district, the population of which had increased somewhat considerably during the preceding few years. As evidence it may be noted that the Golden Lion, which had for several generations been the only licensed house in the district, had an opponent in the Andrew's Arms. The number of entries in the directory had increased from a dozen in 1821 to fifty in 1839. The next decade saw still greater changes, new houses being built in every direction. It was soon evident that as a residential district Collyhurst and Harpurhey were to lose all their charms.

ROCHDALE ROAD.

PART IX.

SOME WELL-KNOWN CHARACTERS.

ELIJAH RIDINGS.

For the greater part of a long lifetime, Elijah Ridings, one of the band of Manchester poets referred to in connection with "Poet's Corner," was associated with the northern portion of the city. He was born on November 27th, 1802, in a cottage in "The Hollow" at Failsworth. His parents, who were silk weavers, had a family of fifteen children, of whom Elijah was the tenth. As was to be expected his school days were few in number, and at a very early age he was kept at home to wind bobbins for use in the silk loom. Elijah being of studious habits managed to considerably improve upon his early education, and as a youth showed a passionate love for poetry, committing many poems to memory. The family removing to Newton Heath he became a teacher in the Sunday School attached to St. George's Church, receiving for his services the usual payment of a shilling per Sunday. Some time afterwards he joined the School library connected with the Unitarian Chapel, Dob Lane, Failsworth, where he made the acquaintance of many other authors. His spare time was filled up with reading, and he tells us that in the week that he first read Bunyan's *Pilgrim's Progress* he wove on his loom six dozen bandanna handkerchiefs. At that time (1817-18) the works of Cobbett and Hone were extensively read by the working classes, and in many districts groups were formed for the purpose of hearing them read. Readers were scarce and Ridings was selected to act as reader for the group to which he belonged. For ten years he was busy with his loom, devoting his leisure time to further study and political work. He was present at Peterloo, and escaped without injury through the intervention of an officer of the 16th Lancers, who called out to him, " Be quick, young man ; this way," and pointing out to him with his sword a way of escape. In 1826 he wrote his first poem, " The Swan," composing it in his mind when working at his loom. He sent the poem to a London correspondent who secured its insertion in *Arliss's Pocket Magazine* for May, 1826. This brought him welcome presents of books from gentlemen personally unknown to him, but who saw merit in his production. In conjunction with John Harper he originated "The Miles Platting Zetetic Society," so named from the Greek word implying " proceeding by inquiry." Out of this arose the " Miles Platting Mechanics Institution," which secured the liberal support of Sir Benjamin Heywood. In 1829 Ridings became an agent for Messrs. Pigot & Co, the compiler of *The National Commercial Directory*, for whom he surveyed Windsor and other districts. After the completion of the work he commenced the delivery of copies in Windsor and the neighbourhood, but his health broke down, and he consulted a doctor, whose verdict was: "Exhausted, you want rest; you ail nothing; there is no disease; you want rest."

He returned home, and after resting for some time, published in 1831 a small collection of poems called *The Village Muse*. He next commenced a day school in Lamb Lane, Collyhurst; but had only been at work a few months when the cholera epidemic came, and his number of pupils was reduced to ten. On May 19th, 1832, he married, and his school failing, he became the landlord of the "Waterman" public house in Butler Street, the sign of which he changed to the "Falstaff and Bardolph." He remained there for three years when the failure of a neighbouring chemical works brought him disaster. At that time Butler Street was unpaved and in wet seasons was almost impassable, the result being that when the works closed his source of trade disappeared. He next tried his hand with bookselling, having a stall in Withy Grove. In those days a number of stalls were ranged alongside the footpath in front of the Seven Stars Inn. A writer in the *Manchester Literary Times* described him as "Sitting patiently by his little stall of books in Withy Grove, with his pale, intelligent face, crowned by grey hairs, though little beyond the midway of life—a quiet and amiable expression, with just such a ray of humour playing about his lips, as you would anticipate after reading what he has written—waiting patiently the fortunes of the day, and thankful by honest industry to make all things meet. The same spirit is found throughout his writings—a spirit of contentment and confidence, warmth of feeling, hopeful but not boisterous, and a bubbling over of humour which he feels no disposition to repress."

Ridings was also noteworthy as having been the last of the Manchester bellmen. This was immediately before he took to book-selling—which he adopted when his office was abolished. He was, take him for all in all, a man of a type becoming gradually rarer. Although compelled to work often for little more than a mere pittance, he always found consolation in the companionship of books; and was never more pleased than when engaged in pointing out the beauties of a favourite author to some young reader, eager for information and enlightenment. Although poor, he nobly did his duty as a citizen, and as such is worthy of remembrance by Manchester men. It is in order that I may do something to prevent his name from being forgotten that I have drawn special notice to him and his work. He died on October 18th, 1872, and was interred in Harpurhey Cemetery, a verse from his poem, the "Evening Star," being inscribed on his gravestone.

"My evening star, my evening star,
Enthroned within thy ebon car,
That smiles on me and lonely things,
While my rapt spirit heavenward springs,
Look down, look down, when I am gone,
With that mild ray that on me shone;
Look down on my dear children twain,
When I no more with them remain;
And may they keep the path of right,
True as thy constant rule of light;
And when my spirit flies afar,
Shine on my grave, my evening star."

BENJAMIN BRIERLEY.

Another well-known resident of the district of more

recent times was Ben Brierley, whose works are so familiar to lovers of the Lancashire dialect as to necessitate only a brief reference to him here. Born in a cottage on the Oldham Road at Failsworth in 1825, he was of very humble parentage. It is pleasant to be able to record that unlike many houses that have interesting associations, Brierley's birthplace has not only survived, but is to be identified by means of a small, dark, granite tablet, bearing the inscription: "This Tablet marks the birthplace of Ben Brierley (Ab-o-th'-Yate), the Lancashire author and poet." Like Ridings, Brierley commenced working very early, and like him wound the bobbins to be used by his seniors at the loom. In 1840, having shown a great love for reading, in which he received much help from a book-loving but poor uncle, he was largely instrumental in founding a Mutual Improvement Society, out of which grew the Failsworth Mechanics Institute. He married in 1855. His occupation was that of a handloom weaver which meant that after working long hours at a monotonous trade he drew only small wages. In spite of this he had contrived to so far improve his education, which, so far as ordinary schooling went, had only been of the briefest duration, that when trade went still worse he was able to take up the position of sub-editor of the *Oldham Times*.

About the same time his first literary effort made its appearance, "*A Day Out*" being published in the *Manchester Spectator*. It was reprinted in book form, and was followed by *Bunk Ho*. The two met with a flattering reception and very shortly *Daisy Nook Sketches* made its appearance. As was to be expected work which was so largely dialectical aroused the antipathies of a portion of the London press, and Brierley was subjected to much adverse criticism, but more abuse which did not deserve to be styled criticism. He afterwards wrote a serial story for the *Manchester Weekly Times.* It bore the title of the *Layrock of Langleyside,* and was re-published afterwards in a volume. He sent a copy to the *Athenæum,* in whose columns his earlier ventures into the realms of literature had been denounced, enclosing with it a plainly worded letter. This brought a reply from the editor, Mr. Hepworth Dixon (a Manchester man) who complained of the tone of the letter, and said that he had not seen the notices referred to. The correspondence was published in the columns of the *Athenæum* and Brierley had no further cause for complaint as to the treatment he received at the hands of the critics. He was now fairly launched in literary work, and for a long succession of years he produced the series of sketches, stories and poems that made his name familiar to Lancashire people in all parts of the world.

In addition to writing he, in company with Edwin Waugh, often appeared at public entertainments, when he would amuse those present by his characteristic rendering of some of his productions. He was induced in 1875 to offer himself as a candidate for municipal honours, and was returned for St. Michael's Ward by 2817 votes against 2628 recorded for Mr. R. T. Walker. He occupied the seat for six years, and evidently in that time had experiences that were not entirely satisfactory, for when a few years later I wrote asking him to attend a meeting to be held in support of the candidature of a relative who was standing for another ward he declined to do so saying that he had made a fool of himself on certain past occasions and did not feel inclined to risk repeating the experience. In common with many other persons Brierley lost a greater portion of his savings, which had been invested in a building society, and a testimonial fund was started by his admirers. The result was that in March, 1885, he was presented with a cheque for £650. By his death Lancashire lost one of the best writers who have made the dialect of the county famous. He was buried at the Harpurhey Cemetery amidst the regrets of a large number of representative men. In 1898 a statue of Brierley was unveiled in Queen's Park at the base of which were placed two inscriptions. The one reads: "In my early days there were few schools to help us in the pursuit of learning. If we wanted to climb we had also to make our own ladders," and the second one: "In prose and verse, and in the dialect spoken by themselves, he set forth with great faithfulness and power the life of the working folk of Lancashire."

In concluding these notes on the Rochdale Road district I will mention a few of the earlier representatives that have sat for St. Michael's ward on the City Council. When the first Council was formed in 1838 three notable men were returned for the ward. They were Thomas Potter, who was first Mayor of the borough, was knighted in 1840, and was a great friend to the education movement; Richard Cobden, the champion of Free Trade; and John Brooks, to whom reference is made in another chapter in this volume.

All three were elected Aldermen at the first meeting of the Council, held on December 15th, 1838; and Henry Hilton, Joseph Adshead and Thomas Molineaux were elected to take their places as councillors. Mr. Adshead was well-known as a philanthropist, but failing in business he was succeeded in the Council in September, 1839, by George Wilson, afterwards Chairman of the Anti-Corn Law League. In our time the ward was represented by William Brown, whose electioneering experiences were many and varied, and by Alderman Thomas Worthington, who was first elected to the Council in 1851. He was registrar of births and deaths for St. George's district.

OLDHAM ROAD.

Part I.

WHEN IT WAS KNOWN AS NEWTON LANE.

Newton was of first importance to the town of many centuries ago as forming a portion of the endowment of the Collegiate Church. In the survey of 1320 we read that the Church was endowed with one messuage, with the rectory, eight burgages in Manchester, and all the *villata* of Newton and Curmesholme or Kirkmans hulme, with meadow, wood and pasture. Harland explains that villata meant assemblages of several or many towns or townships. The whole of Newton Heath, therefore, at one time belonged to the Church, and with it was associated Kirkmanshulme, which is still known as Newton Detached. The land was originally dedicated to the Church by John de la Warre when he rebuilt and endowed it. Naturally, therefore, the way to Newton come to be known as Newton Lane and as such it was known until for some reason, not clearly stated, it was changed to Oldham Road. Great Ancoats Street in the same way was known as Ancoats Lane.

As Newton Lane it was known in 1552 when Laurence Langley was ordered to "dyke his ditch anent his fold end in Newton Lane," and again in 1561 George Hall was ordered "to ditch and amend the way or causeway in Newton Lane." In 1566 Robert Marler was ordered "to make a sufficient course at the end of his fold so that the water that cometh down Newton Lane may pass." The water referred to was very probably the river Tib, which formerly rose in a spring situated in a field situated on the west side of Oldham Road near to Hampson Street. It ran for a long distance parallel to the road, but near to where Livesey Street is it turned a little nearer to the road, and ran from there in an almost straight line to New Cross, then down the length of Tib Street, and so on to Gaythorn, where it joins the Medlock. Along Oldham Road it now flows about eight feet below the surface under the footpath. Until it was culverted over about a hundred and twenty years ago, it was an open stream fringed at intervals with overhanging trees.

There are a number of other references in the Court Leet records to Newton Lane, but they do not present any feature of special interest. Another matter is mentioned from time to time which until recently was shrouded in mystery. I refer to Barlow Cross or Barlow's Cross. One reference to it was made on April 11th, 1587, when complaint was made that an encroachment had been made at Barlow Crosse by William Bolton's house, "whereby the water course of the ditch cannot pass, but greatly hurtful to the highway. It is evident that the stream ran past the cross, and that stream was very probably the river Tib. My friend, Mr. G. H. Rowbotham, has investigated the matter, and the conclusion he has arrived at has been printed in Henry Taylor's *Lancashire Crosses and Holy Wells*. It is stated that Barlow Cross stood on the site of the New Cross. The New Cross as shown in Laurent's plan was built early in the eighteenth century, and was removed in 1819. Suicides were formerly buried at cross roads with a stake driven through the body. Thus we read that in 1746 John Rowbotham, having poisoned himself, was buried at Barlow Cross; that in 1808 a servant woman, having committed suicide, was buried at New Cross; and that in April, 1753, when an ostler at the Saracen's Head hanged himself, the jury ordered "that the body was to be drawn on a sledge, and buried with all clothes on, and to have a stake driven through the body."

Another reference to those early days must be noted. In 1588 a raid was made upon a cottage in Newton Lane, and a printing press was seized and destroyed. The press belonged to Robert Waldegrave, a man of good family and education, who about 1580 commenced the printing and publishing of Puritan tracts. This was distasteful to the Government, and after the appearance of a tract entitled *A Lamentable Complaint of the Commonalitie,* he was imprisoned. After his release he resumed operations, and in 1588 he printed *The State of the Church of England laid open in a Conference.* It was ordered "that the said books be burnte, and the said presse, letters, and printing stuffe defaced and made unserviceable." Hitherto Waldegrave had confined his operations to London, but he now began moving up and down the country carrying a portable press with him. In due course he arrived in Manchester, and set up his press in a cottage in Newton Lane. It is said that the cottage was one of two that stood in a garden on the right hand side of the road about a hundred yards from the corner of Ancoats Lane. He was engaged in printing copies of another tract *Has any more Work for the Cooper*, when he was surprised by the appearance of Lord Derby, who at that time lived at the College. "The press and letters were taken away. The press, being timber, was sawn and hewed in pieces, the ironwork being battered and made unserviceable; his letters melted, with cases and other tools defaced (by John Woolfe, alias Machiavel, beadle of the stationers, and most tormenting executioner of Waldegrave's goods), and he himself for ever deprived of printing again, having a wife and six small children." Such is the account given of the occurrence in a latter Marprelate Tract. From Manchester Waldegrave went to Edinburgh, where he became the King's Printer, but when James succeeded to the English crown in 1605, he returned to London.

The Newton Chapel, built about 1573, was one of the minor chapels erected in different parts of the parish of Manchester for the accommodation of the residents of the various districts, who were thereby prevented the necessity of the journey to the Collegiate Church in order to join in Divine Service. The building was enlarged in 1738 and was rebuilt in 1814; and is now known as All Saint's Church. It is beyond the radius intended to be covered by these volumes, but a few lines may be devoted to several notes concerning it, written by an old resident who remembered the building as it was more than a century ago. He wrote: "Newton Chapel was an ancient brick building, with stone steps outside the edifice to ascend to the gallery and with a clay or earth floor." He could well remember carrying rushes from the rush-cart to lay on the floor of the church; and referred to the old school falling into decay, which necessitated rebuilding, during which time the church was used as a schoolhouse. In the Greaves' Collection are two sketches to which I have previously referred, but in order to make the present story of the evolution of a great thoroughfare more complete I must briefly describe them here.

To the Manchester man of to-day Oldham Road is a wide thoroughfare bounded through its entire length by rows of shops and houses, behind which are situated narrow streets, squalid courts, jerry-built cottages, mills and workshops, with scarcely a trace of brightness to relieve the dull monotony of the prevailing grey and gloom. One cannot realise that within the memory of many still living no further away from New Cross than Butler Street open fields could be seen, and that going back a century, Newton Lane was in truth a pleasant and country lane. In the two views to which I have referred we have glimpses of the lane when it was in that condition. In the first one drawn in 1734 we see a broad thoroughfare fringed by hedgerows. The view is taken from the site of the New Cross and at the corner of Newton Lane and Ancoats Lane is a double fronted cottage which a footnote tells us was the "Iron Dish and Cob of Coal." A little further up the lane is another cottage; and on the opposite side of the lane a woman is represented drawing water from a well or pit. Beyond the second cottage was a footpath that led across the fields to the colliery at Bradford. The second picture is undated. In it we see the New Cross, which consisted of a high stone pillar surmounted by a cross. From the cross a number of market stalls extended up the lane. They were removed in 1821. On both sides of the road houses had been built and a larger building with the sign of the "Crown and Kettle" occupies the site of the earlier cottage.

A licensed house still stands at the corner occupied a hundred and seventy years ago by the "Iron Dish and Cob of Coal."

As our aim in these volumes is to give illustrations of the various phases our city's history has seen, we must include in our review of Newton Lane references to two incidents that caused some excitement in the district more than a century ago. In 1798 a man named George Russell was executed on Newton Heath for robbing the bleaching croft of Mr. Shorrocks, near Scotland Bridge. The second note is an extract from the *Gentleman's Magazine*, wherein we read that "On the 29th (March, 1788), a most daring murder and robbery was committed near Miles Platting, on the person of Mr. Worthington, the York carrier, who had scarcely left the house where he had stayed to drink than he was shot dead, and his watch and chain taken from him; though so near three men on the road before him as to be heard to beg for life."

With these glimpses of Newton Lane we leave it only to renew our acquaintance with it under another name.

OLDHAM ROAD.

Part II.

THE ROAD AS IT WAS SIXTY YEARS AGO.

Sixty years ago the length of Oldham Road from New Cross to Butler Street was pretty much what it is to-day with two rather important exceptions. In the first place the sites of the model dwellings were occupied by cottages and shops, and in the second place in front of many of the cottages near to Butler Street were gardens which in summer times were gay with flowers. To-day a few gardens remain between there and Osborne Street, but their contents have a very grimy appearance; and although even in this state they provide a pleasant relief from the prevailing bricks and mortar, they are very inferior in every respect to their predecessors of sixty years ago. Behind the houses on the right hand side of the road in this section, the whole of the land was built upon; and on the opposite side of the road there was the Oldham Road Station, and adjoining it was St. George's Church, which was immediately surrounded by open land. A portion of the land now occupied by the potato market was unbuilt upon, although a little distance further up the road more building had been done, Apollo, Davidson, and other streets being pretty well built up.

From Butler Street to Lamb Lane much of the front land had been covered, but here the resemblance with the present ceases, for behind most of the houses were open fields. Between Edward Street and Newton Brook was an extensive brickfield, along one side of which ran the open brook. Near to Lowe Street there were several ropewalks, and the name of Cow Lane served to remind residents of the time, not many years earlier, when the whole of the land thereabouts was devoted to agricultural purposes. At the corner of Lamb Lane there was a toll bar, and up the lane, just past the station, was Whitworth Hall, and a little further on Collyhurst Lodge, both of which mansions were surrounded by gardens. Lamb Lane, which ended in a field path leading to the smithy on Rochdale Road, was only partially built up on the right hand side, there being three or four houses on the opposite side. The field path in several cases followed the line of field hedges, and the pedestrian of to-day passing along will be reminded of this by the way in which it turns first to the right and then to the left. Modern made roads are straight, those that have become roads as the result of gradual evolution are usually crooked. At the corner of Hulme Hall Lane there was a bowling green, and down the lane was Hulme Hall. With this exception and with the exception of a group of houses that stood on the canal bank, there were no buildings until the river was crossed. Past Lamb Lane the buildings on the road side became fewer until Newton Heath was reached. On our way thither we should have passed Monsall Lane, another pleasant resort for a ramble, in the course of which the few houses that were passed served to act as landmarks. First, after passing under the railway line there was Newton Heath

Brewery built on the site of an old farm; then came Hardy's Fold standing in a field on the right, and near to was Hardy's Well. Two fields further on was Monsall House, and the only other building between there and Moston Brook was the Monsall Dye Works. Down Grimshaw Lane was the National School, and two or three cottages standing in isolated situations. Ten Acres Lane was a comparatively straight lane in which there was only one cottage until Baguley Fold, a picturesque little settlement, was reached. Looking across the fields the eye would see Cheetham Fold with its cotton mill, Scotland Hall, and a little further away Culcheth Hall standing in a beautifully wooded park. Beyond Ten Acres Lane it is not our intention to travel; but sufficient has been said to show how great have been the changes in little more than half a century in this part of the city. Sixty years ago, standing at the corner of the lane, about two miles from St. Ann's Square, the traveller was surrounded by fields, and in the summer time he would see farming operations being carried on all around him. To-day he is in the centre of a thickly populated district, with dirt, smoke, evil smells, and noise all around. The change for the worse, from the picturesque point of view, could not easily have been more complete, and as one realises it we comprehend what some of the disadvantages of civilisation and commercial prosperity mean in an industrial district.

The preceding fifty years had seen great changes, but changes not so great as those introduced during the sixty years that have passed since 1848. Fifty years before Shudehill pits were undrained and extended to New Cross, and beyond the pits were open fields. It was the same up Newton Lane. Fields and an occasional cottage were passed until Foundry Street was reached, and from there forward for some distance, although streets were laid out, very little building had been done. The site of the railway station and the potato market were open land, but before Butler Lane was reached the lane had assumed a purely rural aspect. There were two rows of cottages with gardens in front, and behind were corn fields. On the opposite side of our thoroughfare the signs of approaching changes were many. Much of the land bounded by Newton Lane, Butler Lane, Union Street, and Ancoats Lane had been laid out in streets. Many of the streets had been named, but very little building had been done.

The changes referred to seem to have commenced about 1775, in which year a conveyance was made by Henry Legh and George Legh, of High Legh, Cheshire, to Thomas Bound, bricklayer, of Manchester, of certain lands near Newton Lane end, and consisting of a field called "The Great Croft," which was bounded on two of its sides by Newton Lane and Ancoats Lane. Two years later Bound sold a portion of the land to Thomas Hodkinson, of Didsbury, and very probably building operations began immediately. Amongst the street names thereabouts the names of these early owners are perpetuated; thus in Henry Street, George Street and George Leigh Street we are reminded of the well-known Cheshire family. Cornwall Street had a similar origin, for George Legh married Anna Maria, daughter and heiress of Francis Cornwall, Baron of Burford. The Manchester bricklayer was remembered for a century in the street name which at different periods was spelled Bound, Boond, Boon and Bond Street, but was in later years renamed Luna Street.

From this early record we can trace the beginning of the change which has converted a country lane into a long street, bounded by houses and other buildings, and connected our city with Oldham by means of bricks and mortar. And all this has been done in about a hundred and thirty years.

BUTLER LANE AND BUTLER STREET.

On Laurent's plan we see Butler Lane, now identified by the more prosaic name of Butler Street, depicted as a pleasant country lane. Hedgerows lined both sides and at the corner of Newton Lane was a house to which there was apparently attached outbuildings, and a garden. It is more than probable that it was a farm the tenant of which would farm the land which, extended along both sides of the lane. Near to where the canal bridge is to-day the Shooters Brook was crossed, and close by were several houses together with a small plantation. The continuation of the lane is marked "In Holt Town," and we also have Bradford Road duly depicted, many trees apparently growing in its hedgerows. A field path leads from New Islington, then very different from the New Islington of to-day, and in the fields through which it passes were several small morasses in which rushes are depicted as growing. Houses were few and far between in Butler Lane and its neighbourhood in the closing decade of the eighteenth century.

Shooters Brook to which reference has been made, rose in the fields that adjoined the Gleden coal pit.

After passing through Gagg's fields it joined Newton Brook just before passing under Butler Lane. From there it flowed through the fields of New Islington near to where it widened out for a short distance. Near to Ancoats Lane it gave the name to a short street, and a little distance further on it ran under Ancoats Lane by a bridge known as Shooters Brook Bridge. Flowing in the direction of London Road it passed through the fields now covered by Store Street, and the adjacent buildings. London Road sloped down on both sides of the bridge that crossed the little stream near to Store Street, the portion of the thoroughfare on the Ardwick side being Bank Top, whilst that on the opposite side was known as Shooters Brow. It was in the fields on the bank of the brook that the Rev. William Bourne, one of the ministers connected with the Collegiate Church preached during the plague visitation of 1605. After passing under London Road the stream bore somewhat to the right, passing across the end of Brook Street. Where Minshull Street crosses were then fields and near to there a small plantation of trees grew on the right hand bank. Running open for its entire length, the stream next passed along the bottoms of the gardens of some cottages that stood in Aurora Place, the site of which is now merged into Whitworth Street near to the corner of Princess Street. Close by, at Garratt, Shooters Brook lost itself in the Medlock. A century ago the brook was an open stream of clear water. To-day, culverted over and lost to sight, it is nothing better than a minor drain, and beyond the fact of two short streets being named after it there is nothing to be seen to-day that reminds us of its existence.

Returning now to Butler Street we may make a note concerning Gagg's fields, which have been already mentioned. The fields took their name from the family who for several generations farmed the land thereabouts. To members of later generations of Manchester people the name was familiar on account of the musical talents of some of the family.

Another Butler Lane name that should be remembered was that of Antrobus. For several generations the family lived in a small cottage on the site of which the Brown Cow public house was afterwards built. The first member of the family of whom we have any record was Philip Antrobus, who was celebrated as a clock maker. Occasionally one may see an old grandfather's clock bearing his name, although they must be only few in number. He died in 1762 and was buried at the Collegiate Church. His son, also Philip, continued the clock-making business but also did a little farming. He died in 1820 and was buried at St. Mary's Church. In those days Butler Lane was a very quiet thoroughfare; and for a long time the only near neighbours to the Antrobuses were the Gaggs family, whose half timbered farm stood almost opposite to theirs. One night burglars broke into the clock maker's cottage and tied Mr. Antrobus in his chair whilst they ransacked the place. The third generation of the family was represented by William Antrobus, who was the first landlord of the Brown Cow. He died in 1847, leaving a maiden sister, who died about thirty years ago. In this way we can link up the Butler Lane of 1760 and the Butler Street of a century later.

Bennett Street Sunday School, Manchester.

OLDHAM ROAD.

PART III.

BENNETT STREET SUNDAY SCHOOL.

Few institutions in the city have exerted a greater influence for good during the last century, or are better known than is Bennett Street Sunday School. Founded more than a century ago, unlike many similar institutions it is as vigorous in its operations to-day as it has been any time during its long career. When it first commenced is somewhat doubtful, for records of its earliest days are very few and far between. So far as can be ascertained the scholars first met in a room in Primrose Street in 1801 or thereabouts. It appears certain that David Stott, the founder, had a Sunday School there in 1805. The movement prospered, and in 1808 a move was made to a larger building in George Leigh Street. At that time there were 726 scholars on the books, and these were instructed by David Stott and Henry Young and a staff of sixteen teachers. In 1811 the school was affiliated with St. Clement's Church, Stevenson Square, but in 1824 the management of it was transferred to St. Paul's Church, Turner Street. About midway between these dates in consequence of the great increase in the number of scholars a move was made to the building still standing in Bennett Street. The cost of erection was £2524 and the opening took place on December 13th, 1818. As proof of the popularity of the school it is only necessary to mention that in 1814 there were no fewer than 1905 scholars, with a staff of thirty teachers and eighty monitors.

David Stott was the great controlling force in connection with the school, and for many years after his death the institution was well known as Stott's School, and Bennett Street, or St. Paul's. It is therefore necessary that something should be said in this connection concerning the man. He was born at Ripponden, near Halifax, in 1779, his father, Thomas Stott being a farmer and woollen manufacturer. In 1790 the family came to Manchester, and David Stott was sent to the Grammar School, where he remained for three years. He entered the employment of Thomas Worthington, a smallware and silk manufacturer of 50 and 51 High Street, and who added the making of umbrellas just at the time that they were becoming popular. Mr. Stott soon obtained the fullest confidence of his employer, and was sent on many responsible journeys. In those days, before the advent of the railway, and when banking operations were conducted on somewhat primitive lines; and Mr. Stott often went to London by stagecoach, carrying with him large sums of money to pay for the goods that he was commissioned to purchase. In the early days of the umbrella industry cane was used for making the frames, and Mr. Stott often went to Spain to purchase cane. He was a man of singular integrity and honour as is illustrated by the following story. It was customary at Worthington's and other manufactories to impose upon workpeople penalties for all kinds of complaints, real and imaginary; and as a consequence the operatives rarely received their full wages. The deductions made at Worthington's did not succeed in securing the object aimed at, and Mr. Stott was asked for an explanation. His reply was: "If you want your servants to be honest to you, you must be honest to them." He was never again troubled on the question. He died on February 26th, 1848 and was buried in Bowdon churchyard. On the occasion of his death a memorial quarto sheet was issued, having a woodcut of the school at the head, and containing some memorial verses to which the author's name was not attached.

In 1831 Benjamin Braidley issued the first volume of *Sunday School Memorials*, consisting of a series of biographies of worthies who had been connected with the school. In 1880 a second volume was issued, and in 1904 an edition de luxe was published under the editorship of Messrs. George Milner and B. A. Redfern. From the preface to the 1831 volume we gather some interesting information concerning the work of the school at that time. There was a circulating library of 650 volumes, which was begun with a subscription list that amounted to over £100. There was a tract association and a Bible association, a writing club, a sick society, and a funeral society. The last named societies, which soon became very popular, were originated by Mr. Stott. Mr. Braidley was an active worker in connection with the school. For a long time he was co-superintendent along with Mr. Stott. He was boroughreeve of Manchester in 1831 and 1832, and in 1835 he twice contested Manchester in the Conservative interest. He died in 1845.

In the records of the school we find that the first time that Whitsuntide festivities were arranged was 1827 when the teachers went to Bradford-cum-Beswick and took tea there on the Thursday, and that on the Friday the scholars were taken to Blackley. In 1851 the jubilee year of the school, Manchester was visited by Queen Victoria, and the scholars of Bennett Street joined in the welcome at Peel Park. No fewer than three thousand children received medals and cups on the occasion. Since then the work of the school has been carried on by succeeding generations of enthusiastic volunteer workers. In 1903 it was found necessary to extend the building and funds were raised for that purpose. The highest contribution was made by Mrs. Hoyle, who gave £1000 in memory of her husband's long connection with the school. In recognition of this generous contribution the extension was named the Hoyle wing, the memorial stone of which was laid by Mrs. Hoyle. As showing the amount of work still done in connection with the school some of the principal branches of effort may be enumerated. In the first place in spite of the greatly increased number of Sunday Schools, and the changes that have emptied many churches, chapels and schools, Bennett Street still has 1500 scholars including 300 adults. The last named fact is notable in connection with the institution for in very many cases the fact that persons have become associated with it in childhood's years is sufficient reason for them retaining their connection with it in later years, and it may be said that the whole of the three hundred adults now attending its classes first commenced visiting the building as tiny toddlers, taken there held by the hand by their elders. The affection shown by the old scholars for their school is remarkable, and in striking contrast to the experience of too many Sunday Schools.

There is a day school attended by over four hundred pupils, and other means of imparting education. The Literary and Educational Society has for many years been regarded as one of the best in the city; and has associated with it an interesting and unique feature. This is the manuscript magazine bearing the title of *Odds and Ends*, which for more than sixty years has been issued annually. As its description denotes it consists of manuscript contributions by members of the school on every conceivable variety of subject. Year by year a fresh volume is issued, and included in it are photographs, pen and ink drawings, water-colour drawings, and other illustrations executed in every case by scholars, teachers or officials. The series, carefully edited and substantially bound, is one of the most treasured possessions of the school. The first volume was edited by George Milner, and every volume issued since has borne his name, although for several years he has been assisted in the duties of editorship by Mr. B. A. Redfern, whose love for his old school is as keen as that of his revered senior. Amongst the many branches of labour undertaken may be enumerated the Free Library, which was commenced in 1813, the Sick and Burial Society, which dates from 1812, and the Penny Bank, which has existed for 56 years. Then there are such organisations as the Band of

Hope, and the Book Club ; and recreation is represented by a Cricket Club, a Chess Club, a Rambling Club, and a Swimming Club. This does not exhaust the list of institutions connected with Bennett Street, and it is doubtful whether greater vitality is displayed by the members of any other Sunday school than is displayed by the members of the well-known Manchester school.

As might have been expected there have been connected with the school during the century that it has had an existence many men and women who have rendered valuable services in various capacities as citizens. The three volumes of memorials just referred to contain notices of men and women who in their lives served their Church and school well and faithfully, and I must refer my readers for particulars of these worthies to the volumes themselves, for they will well repay the trouble of perusal. There are, however, several names that must be mentioned, if only in the briefest possible manner. We have already referred to David Stott and Benjamin Braidley, whose names will be held in reverence so long as the school has an existence. As an outsider, not connected in any way with the school, I should name our veteran citizen, George Milner as being fully entitled to the next place in the school's roll of fame. During a very long life he has been connected with it, and he has been tireless in the manner in which he has served it in almost every official position in turn. Few schools can point to such a magnificent record of service rendered by any person connected with it as can Bennett Street so far as Mr. Milner is concerned. And this has not been all. The veteran worker has intellectual gifts equalled by few, and these he has always freely placed at the service of the school. The half-century's editorship of *Odds and Ends* has been one way in which that service has been rendered; for during the last fifty years Mr. Milner has in a multitude of ways sought to encourage in the young people of the school a study of what is best in the world's literature. It is a safe thing to say that no Manchester citizen of to-day is beloved by a wider range of his fellows than is Mr. Milner; and whenever the time should come for him to remove from this sphere of activity, thousands will experience a deep personal loss. His life has been one long object lesson, which all could with advantage to themselves copy. Other names recur to the memory, but only a few can be mentioned, and these only in the briefest possible manner. There was the Rev. Robert Lamb, who for thirty years held the living of St. Paul's and was untiring in his efforts on behalf of the school. Contemporaneous with him was William Hepworth Dixon, who, born in Ancoats, and employed in his early years in a cotton mill, took up literature as a study, removed to London, became editor of the *Athenæum*, and wrote a number of books which for a time enjoyed a wide popularity. In his childhood's years Dixon was connected with Bennett Street, and it was there that he received the first inspirations that ended in his reaching a high position in the literary world.

Very different as types of men from Hepworth Dixon were two of the school worthies, W. Foster and William Hoyle, who were associated in the foundation of the

Band of Hope. In the early days of the temperance movement these friends took the matter seriously to heart, and were tireless in their efforts to advocate its claims upon all who were interested in social reform. Mr. Hoyle's field for operations was a wide one. Not content with speaking from the platform, he turned his attention to the writing of hymns and songs suitable for singing at temperance gatherings. The Band of Hope movement ever had in him a stalwart friend, and in connection with it he visited every part of the country, and addressed thousands of meetings. In all this he always retained a kindly thought for his old school, and having married a fellow scholar, she, in order to show their joint gratitude for benefits received as a result of their association with it, gave the sum of £1000 towards the extension fund. It was with peculiar pleasure that the writer, although a stranger to all but Mrs. Hoyle, was able on the occasion of the stone-laying to say a few words on her behalf. She died about two months later at Blackpool. Mr. Foster, who was a colleague with Mr. Hoyle in the founding of the Band of Hope was a man of great learning and a musician with considerable talents. Another musician was John Nesbitt, whose son, W. S. Nesbitt, is the conductor of the Manchester Orpheus Musical Society, which commenced in 1897. Growing out of the school and church, the society has always held its rehearsals at Bennett Street, and to-day wherever male choral singing is cultivated, the name and fame of the Manchester Orpheus Male Voice Choir is known. Recently the school lost an old adherent in Alderman Grantham, who showed an active interest in many of the movements connected with the school.

There are many other names that might be mentioned, but enough has been said to show how great the work has been that has been achieved in connection with the old school. As an institution it has more than justified its existence; and during the last century there must have been many thousands of citizens who have been indebted to it for inspiration in all things that make for sobriety and good citizenship.

OLDHAM ROAD.

PART IV.

ELIJAH DIXON.

It is more than thirty years since Elijah Dixon, one of the most stalwart of the little band of reformers who, in the early part of the last century, championed the cause of the workers of England, passed away. His career was in more respects than one very remarkable, and no account of the growth of our city during the last century would be complete without some description of the man and his work.

Dixon was born at Kirkburton-in-Wooldale, Yorkshire, on October 23rd, 1790. His father, after enjoying a considerable amount of prosperity as a manufacturer, encountered very severe reverses, lost his money, and was compelled to seek employment. In his search for work he found his way to Manchester where he obtained a situation as a fustian cutter, an occupation never characterised by a high rate of wages. His children got work in various cotton mills in Ancoats, Elijah beginning as a "scavenger," and after years of industrious application he became a "piecer." A lover of books, he read all that came in his way, and as a youth commenced taking an intelligent interest in the various political agitations inaugurated in that stormy period of our country's history by Sir Francis

Burdett and Major Cartwright. It is not surprising to learn, therefore, that the young enthusiastic reformer was present at Peterloo. His activity was such that the attention of the Government spies was drawn to his movements, and one morning, whilst following his occupation at Houldsworth's mill in Newton Street, only recently pulled down, he was arrested by a King's messenger and a deputy constable, and lodged in the New Bailey prison. Doubly ironed he was sent to London, treated on the way kindly enough by one of his keepers, but with much harshness by the deputy constable, who persistently refused to allow the irons to be removed until the coach was within a few miles of London. Arrived there he was arraigned before Lord Sidmouth, and was sentenced to eight weeks imprisonment in Tothill Fields prison. Returning to Manchester he resumed his occupation in the mill, Mr. Houldsworth, although a pronounced Tory in politics, recognising in the young reformer a good workman. When the Government proposed to bring in a bill for the repeal of the Act for suspending the Habeas Corpus Act, a number of reformers of Manchester petitioned the House of Commons, declaring the falsehood of the allegations on which the suspension had taken place, and praying that redress might be afforded to those who had suffered injustice and wrong during that disturbed and anxious time. Amongst the petitioners was Elijah Dixon, whose petition ran: "That the petitioner was, on the 12th March, 1817, whilst following his lawful occupation, apprehended on a warrant issued by Lord Sidmouth, and carried to London in double irons, and was on the 15th of the same month committed to Tothill Fields Bridewell by the same lord on the suspicion of high treason, and there detained until the 13th of November, although the same lord must, or might have known that he was perfectly innocent of the crime imputed to him. The petitioner, therefore, prays that the House will please to consider the justice of making the said noble lord responsible for the loss of time to the petitioner and for the injuries which his family has suffered in consequence of his long, unjust, and unredressed imprisonment. He also prays that they will be pleased to adopt such a reform in the election of members to serve in the House as shall give to each man a feeling sense that he is represented, and enable him once more proudly to boast of our glorious constitution in King, Lords, and Commons." Needless to say Dixon received no compensation for the indignity and injustice to which he had been subjected.

Having a desire for greater freedom, he gave up his situation in the mill, and commenced trading on his own account. His first effort was as a milk dealer, and he began a "round" in Ancoats, the milk being carried in cans slung over a donkey's back. On his first morning, just as he was ready to start, he went indoors for a moment, leaving the donkey already laden at the door. Whilst he was away a wasp attacked the donkey and stinging it, caused it to roll over in the street. Needless to say the milk was lost, and when Dixon appeared on the scene, he surveyed the disaster with all the equanimity he could command. He gave up the idea of being a milk dealer, sold the donkey and cans, and tried his fortune as a pedlar.

Not meeting with much encouragement he tried his hand at pill box making. In this he was successful, and before very long he added to it the making of lucifer matches, then quite a novelty. He soon found that he was on the right lines and his business grew with amazing rapidity. At first a day or two's travelling per week sufficed to meet his requirements, but he gradually increased the area over which he worked, and devoted the whole of his time to the collection of orders. In later years the operations of his business kept half a dozen travellers going. The match-making business thus initiated in 1841 was known successively as Elijah Dixon ; Dixon, Son & Co. ; Dixon & Nightingale ; and Dixon, Son, & Evans.

Whilst developing a growing business Mr. Dixon devoted a considerable amount of time and energy to other matters. Temperance, co-operation, and the abolition of slavery were three of the great causes that secured his support and advocacy ; whilst as a teacher and preacher his services in Sunday School and Church work were long continued. Popular education found in him an enthusiastic supporter, and his voice was often raised on behalf of the various matters forming the programme of the Liberal party of the day.

A man of remarkable vigour, he retained until his latest years his full powers. Born in 1790, he was eighty-five years of age when he made his last ascent of Snaefell in the Isle of Man. A year later, on July 26th, 1876, he died after a few days' illness.

A few words may be said now concerning the business concern that Mr. Dixon founded in 1841. It developed so rapidly that in 1850 about four hundred and fifty men, women and children were employed. The timber yard was over two acres in extent, and it was nothing unusual to have ten thousand pounds' worth of timber in stock. Gradually there grew up a general timber trade alongside that of match making, but in 1880 a severance between the two took place, the match business being disposed of to Messrs. Bell and Company, and was finally absorbed by Messrs. Bryant and May Limited. The timber trade is now carried on under the title of

GEORGE EVANS AND SONS.

The works cover five acres of land, and an extensive business is done as timber merchants, steam saw-millers, and joiners. George Evans, who married a daughter of Mr. Dixon, has been succeeded by his four sons in the proprietorship of the business. One of these, W. T. Evans, acted as a member of the Prestwich Board of Guardians for some years, whilst his brother, George, took a prominent part in local affairs, was elected a councillor for Newton Heath when the district was added to the city, and was afterwards appointed first alderman for the ward.

Few business concerns in the city have been evolved from such humble beginnings as has that of Messrs. Geo. Evans & Sons, for Elijah Dixon, the ex-cotton operative, only took up the pill box making trade out of which grew that of match making, after he had failed to make a living as a pedlar; and it may also be noted that the business has grown as the district in which it is located has developed. When Dixon began the making of matches Newton Heath and Miles

Platting were semi-suburban in character. Now they form one great manufacturing area along with the remainder of the city, and the person on the look-out for a suburban residential retreat must look for it beyond the boundaries of Newton Heath.

It may be noted in closing that in the Manchester Directory Elijah Dixon is described as a shopkeeper carrying on business at 42 Great Ancoats Street, and that in 1838 he was at 5, Dixon Street, Woodward Street, Ancoats, where he kept a shop. Another entry shows that he was in partnership with David Ridgway under the style of Dixon & Ridgway, pill box and syringe manufacturers, and plaster spreaders, at New Islington.

OLDHAM ROAD.

PART V.

THREE SCHOOLS.

THE LANCASTERIAN SCHOOL.

One of the first attempts made to extend education in the city was commenced in 1810 in Marshall Street, Oldham Road. The school was associated with the work of Joseph Lancaster concerning whom, although not a Manchester man, a few words must be said. Lancaster, who was born in Southwark in 1778, became a schoolmaster when only twenty years old. He gave a grounding in the three R's and imparted a knowledge of the Bible, though he "carefully abstained from associating religion with any sect or party." He usually charged a fee of four pence per week, but the payment of a fee was optional, as was shown by a sign over his front door to the effect, "All that will may send their children, and have them educated freely; and those that do not wish to have education for nothing may pay for it, if they please." He struck out new lines and adopted the system of teaching by monitors. At the same time a rival educationalist obtained much public attention and support; and as a result of the feud that arose between the two parties there came into existence two organised movements, the National Society, that supported Dr. Bell, and the British and Foreign School Society that supported Joseph Lancaster. This was in 1811. The fame of Lancaster's school spread far and wide, and it was visited by foreign princes, ambassadors, peers, bishops, and archbishops, everyone in turn being struck by the perfect order that prevailed. It became the fashion to support the Lancasterian system of education, and schools based upon the system were opened in different parts of the country. It should be noted that an attempt to extend the system to the teaching of agriculture ended in failure. A large piece of land was placed at Lancaster's disposal by the Duke of Somerset, and the boys were divided into classes, each of which was in the charge of a monitor. Everything was to be done by word of command. At the order "Prepare to dig," the boys, arranged in lines, grounded their spades, and prepared for work; and at the command "Dig," the spade was pressed down; a third order, "Turn," intimating that the soil was to be turned and broken. The experiment was a failure, but the success of Lancaster's elementary education system was undoubted.

In Manchester the experiment was first tried in a room in Lever Street, and as a result of the success that attended it a school was planned and built in Marshall Street, Oldham Road. At the time (1809) the people of the country were celebrating the jubilee of George III. and it was decided that in Manchester one portion of the celebration should take the form of opening a free Lancasterian day school. Subscriptions were willingly sent in, and in 1812 the foundation stone of the school that was to accommodate a thousand scholars was laid. The opening day was July 26th, 1813; and in this connection it is interesting to read the opinions expressed at the time concerning what was undoubtedly the greatest step in the direction of national education that had up to then been made in the country. One writer said: "To this school every stranger who visits Manchester should repair during the hours of instruction, that they may enjoy the sight of a living picture, which Benevolence will pant to see copied in every town in the kingdom."

The amount of support accorded to the school varied very considerably from year to year; thus in 1827 the subscriptions amounted to £2484, but on the other hand, in 1838 they only reached £374. For many years it was the only day school in the neighbourhood, and was constantly full. About 1854 the first Government grant was received. So far as the teaching staff was concerned it may be noted that for many years, although there were 1200 scholars in attendance, there were only two masters and one mistress engaged, the remainder of the work being done by monitors. In 1860 the teaching staff consisted of one master, three assistants, and eight pupil teachers for the boys; and of one mistress and nine pupil teachers for the girls. The advent of the School Board system caused a falling off in the attendance at and the support given to the school, and in 1880 it was transferred to the School Board.

GERMAN STREET SUNDAY SCHOOL AND ST. PETER'S CHURCH.

Everett in his *Panorama of Manchester*, published in 1834, says of the Sunday Schools under the Established Church in the Oldham Road area that "St. Paul's being the district where such institutions appear to be most needed has four schools, viz., No. 1 in Gun Street, Ancoats, 85 scholars. This building was given by Mr. Simeon Newton, and is the first that was ex-exclusively appropriated to this purpose. No. 2 in Copperas Street, 258 scholars. No. 3 in German Street, 1330 scholars. This school was for many years held in a garret in Jersey Street, but in 1826 the present building was erected, at a cost of £2300 to accommodate 1300 scholars. No. 4 in Bennett Street is the largest Sunday School in the town. It was built in 1818. It consists of four rooms, 60 feet by 36, and comfortably accommodates 2687 scholars. Total in St. Paul's district, 4360 scholars."

We have already dealt with the Bennett Street school. Our concern now is with the one that formerly stood in German Street. The school was commenced about 1801 in Dean Street but was removed afterwards to Jersey Street. It was often known as Young's school, and the reason for this is not difficult to discover. John Young, a spinner in a cotton mill in Ancoats, was very much interested in the Sunday School movement, and for more than half a century was a worker in connection with it. He began teaching in a Sunday School opened in a small room in Pool Fold, in 1786. About the opening of the last century he was living in Dean Street, and commenced teaching either in a room in his own house or in one adjacent to it. Out of this arose the German Street School which was built in 1826. After serving as master of the school for many years he was appointed a visitor, and occupied that position when he died in March, 1843, in his seventy ninth year. As the population of the district increased the Church of St. George was not sufficient to accommodate the would-be worshippers. Sunday evening services were therefore commenced at German Street, and round the building as a nucleus there gradually gathered the machinery of a new parish. At length a district was assigned to it, a clergyman was appointed, and on June 25th, 1859, the foundation stone of St. Peter's Church was laid, the building being consecrated by Bishop Lee on January 14th, 1860.

THE GUN STREET SCHOOL AND ITS FOUNDER.

The Gun Street school referred to by Everett as the first building exclusively devoted to Sunday School purposes, was a cottage purchased by Simeon Newton. On the front wall was a tablet bearing the inscription: "The gift of Simeon Newton, for the use of Sunday Schools. Nov. 12th, 1788." The story of the foundation was traced by the indefatigable John Owen, and is worth repeating. "Simeon Newton was the second son and third child of Simeon Newton, of Manchester, who was married at the Collegiate Church in 1731 to Dorothy Shore. Their son, Simeon, was baptised at the Collegiate Church, July 4th, 1736, and was buried there on January 1st, 1795. *The Manchester Mercury* of that date had the following notice of his decease: 'Died, on Monday, Mr. Simeon Newton, generally respected by all who knew him; the poor in the neighbourhood will long feel his loss.' Many years ago I was told by an aged relative who had some recollections of him, that Simeon being at sea—but whether as a sailor or passenger has slipped my memory—the vessel was captured by a French cruiser, and an armed force was put on board to conduct the prize to a French port. The captured party, perceiving that they were not very vigilantly guarded, rose in the night and succeeded in turning the tables on their captors, and regaining possession of the vessel, which they brought safely to England. As a thanksgiving for his escape from a French prison, Newton, out of his share of the prize money, disposed of a portion in the erection of the Sunday School in Gun Street."

Such was the romantic story of the origin of Manchester's first Sunday School building. In the Manchester directory for 1788 we have the entry: "Newton Simeon, brick maker, Ancoats Lane." This had reference to the worthy we have been referring to.

OLDHAM ROAD.

Part VI.

A FEW NOTABLE EVENTS.

FOOD RIOTS.

National affairs in England were productive of much excitement and irritation in 1796. The war in which we were engaged was not popular; and a scarcity of corn resulting in almost prohibitive prices so far as the working classes were concerned, caused popular feeling to rise to fever point. Poverty, starvation, and discontent seemed to be preparing England for a repetition of that rising that changed the current of French history. Locally, the authorities resorted to many expedients for meeting the situation caused thereby. In July an order was issued that all public houses be closed by seven in the evening, and that all private persons appearing in the streets after nine o'clock should be compelled to give an account of themselves. On the 29th of the same month several gentlemen were examining the weights in the potato market when a dispute arose. A crowd collected, windows were broken, and the troops were sent for. In this way the crowd was dispersed, but the following morning they reassembled in Newton Lane. Loads of meal were taken by force and distributed; several shops were attacked, and great excitement existed until the soldiers were again called in.

THE FIRST TEETOTAL SOCIETY IN ENGLAND.

In 1834 Dr. R. B. Grindrod, who is notable as having been the first medical man to join the teetotal cause, which he had done in 1833, held a series of temperance meetings at Miles Platting, and as a result he formed a teetotal society, at one of whose gatherings the Rev. F. Beardsall signed the pledge. Mr. Beardsall was a Baptist minister who was president of the Young Mens' Mutual Improvement Society, formed in connection with Dr. M'All's chapel in Mosley Street. It is said that the Miles Platting society was the first public and exclusively teetotal society formed in England. The success of the movement was such that a building was erected by the Society for its sole use. A few months after the opening of the building the flooring of a meeting room gave way during a temperance meeting. Two persons were killed and seventy were injured. Dr. Stanley, who afterwards became Bishop of Norwich, visited the sufferers, and became an abstainer, although he resumed the moderate use of wine afterwards by order of his medical attendant.

A CURIOUS VERDICT.

On January 28th, 1845, a serious accident occurred at the engine house of the Manchester and Leeds Railway at Miles Platting. The locomotive engine " Irk," which had been built from the designs of George Robert Stephenson, and which had run some 76,000 miles, exploded, killing three men. The coroner's jury placed a deodand of £500 on the engine. The word deodand is so rarely used that it will perhaps be excusable for me to point out that a deodand is any personal chattel which is the immediate occasion of the death of a rational creature, and, for that reason, given to God, or forfeited to be applied to pious or charitable use. The engine being valued at £500, the Company were therefore required to devote that sum to charitable purposes. In 1846 the absurd law was repealed by Parliament.

THE SUPPRESSION OF CHARTISM.

In tracing the history of a community we are compelled to deal with a variety of subjects. It thus comes about that from time to time reference is made to political movements that have in their time exerted great influence upon the residents of the city. About sixty years ago Chartism was passing through the death struggle, and in Manchester as elsewhere the final scenes were being enacted. For the guidance of my younger readers I will recount the political aims of the Chartists, without expressing any opinion thereon. They demanded 1st, Manhood Suffrage; 2nd, Annual Parliaments; 3rd, Vote by Ballot; 4th, Abolition of the Property Qualification for Members of Parliament; 5th, Payment of Members; 6th, Equal Electoral Districts. These were claimed to be essentials in the Charter of national freedom, they were called the six points of the Charter, and the advocates were called Chartists. There were in Manchester many who sympathised with the movement, and in the Oldham Road and Ancoats districts the adherents were very numerous. During the month of July, 1848, there were many rumours current in the town as to the intentions of the Chartists, and the Irish Confederates, with the result that the magistrates decided to take strong measures to break up the clubs and associations of the two parties. Consequently, on August 3rd a force of three hundred constables assembled at Oldham Road and under the command of Captain Willis and the Superintendents they visited the various clubrooms in the district. Fifteen persons were arrested. On August 22nd some of these, along with Chartist orators and leaders arrested in other districts, were tried at the assizes at Liverpool, and were sentenced to various periods of imprisonment. The incident caused considerable excitement in the Oldham Road district.

AN ALARMING INCIDENT.

The residents of Miles Platting were very much alarmed by an accident that occurred during the violent thunderstorm that broke over Manchester on June 24th, 1874. There was connected with the machine works of Evan Leigh, Son and Company a high chimney which was struck by lightning. The lightning struck the coping of the chimney which was formed of terra cotta, and was forty feet in circumference. About half of this was broken off, and after the lightning entered the chimney it left it again by making a huge hole about twelve yards from the top. The hole was about twelve yards long and was about four yards wide in one part. Pieces of terra cotta and bricks were hurled in all directions, some being found sixty yards away. As a large portion of the roof of the works was demolished it was remarkable that none of the workmen were killed, and only three injured.

ST JOHN'S CHURCH, MILES PLATTING.

The Church of St. John the Evangelist was consecrated by Bishop Prince Lee on December 7th, 1855. The architect was Mr. G. Shaw, and the cost of erection was £5000. The building was brought into prominence about a quarter of a century ago by the ritualistic practices indulged in by the Rev. Sidney Fairthorn Green. The prosecution and imprisonment of this popular and able minister was the only regrettable incident connected with the Bishop Fraser's tenure of office. Apart from his views and actions on the questions of ritual, few ministers of his day were more popular amongst the poorer residents of that part of the city than was Mr. Green. He visited, and as far as his circumstances permitted, assisted those of his poor neighbours, who were the victims of sickness or other forms of misfortune. When circumstances resulted in his imprisonment he was the object of much sympathy on the part of thousands who differed from him on theological matters. It was a matter of sincere regret that it should have fallen to the lot of a Christian leader of the type of Bishop Fraser to take a step which must have caused him much suffering.

OLDHAM ROAD.

PART VII.

A FEW WELL-KNOWN NAMES.

REV. JABEZ BUNTING, D.D.

Perhaps the most notable person whose birth has taken place in Oldham Road was Jabez Bunting, who was born there on May 3rd, 1779, and who was taken by his mother to the Oldham Street Wesleyan Chapel in order that he might receive the blessing of the Rev. John Wesley. Twenty years later the boy grown to man's estate, stood along with twenty-eight others, round the front of the gallery in the same chapel to be admitted into full connection with the Wesleyan Conference as a preacher. For fifty nine years he was a minister in the Wesleyan body, and in the course of that time he occupied every official position in connection with it. As a preacher he was the most effective and popular of his day; his style being pronounced by Robert Hall as " a limpid stream of classic elegance." As a preacher and as a debater no other Wesleyan minister showed such remarkable power as did Mr. Bunting; and this, combined with his great intellectual powers, caused him to be regarded as the most representative man of the Wesleyan Connexion of the first half of the last century. After a life crowded with work and incident he died on June 16th,

1858, at Myddleton Square, London. He was educated by Dr. Percival, and one of his earliest and closest friends was the Rev. Adam Clarke, D.D.

WILLIAM HOLLAND AND SONS.

Rather more than half a century ago William Holland commenced business in a cotton mill situated in the Adelphi, Salford. Its proximity to the river resulted in the lower portions of the building being flooded from time to time as a result of the rapid rising of the stream. These experiences entailed very serious damage to machinery, etc., in addition to inconvenience to business caused by stoppages. Mr. Holland therefore decided to secure a more favourable site, and in 1867 he acquired property at Miles Platting, upon which he built the Victoria Mill. Six years later he added a second mill; each building being seven stories high, 150 feet long, and 135 feet deep. In 1877 the firm commenced spinning "French Cashmere yarns," and very shortly a further mill was erected. Since then various extensions have been made, and as employers of labour, Hollands stand in the very first rank amongst textile manufacturers. In 1872 W. Holland admitted his two sons, Samuel and William Henry, to partnership. It is noteworthy that the three gentlemen have taken an active part in public affairs, the father becoming a magistrate and a member of the Lancashire County Council. William Henry Holland has, however, attained to a higher public position than either his father or his brother. As chairman of the Newton Heath Local Board at the time of the amalgamation with Manchester, he became a candidate for the City Council at the first election and was returned, and was appointed the first Alderman for the ward. Since then he has taken an active interest in national politics and his services as a Member of Parliament and in other ways was fittingly recognised by the conferment of the honour of knighthood upon him a few years ago. He is at all times sympathetic with all movements for social reform, and has in many ways shown his appreciation of the services rendered to the community by the great medical charities of our city.

PETER SPENCE.

Although Newton Heath is beyond the district dealt with in this volume, Mr. Peter Spence was so well-known in connection with many movements for the regeneration of those who have been described as "the submerged tenth," which section is well represented in this part of the city, that a word must be said with reference to him. He was born at Brechin in 1806, and as a youth became interested in social questions. When in later years the temperance question came to the front, he at once gave it all the support he could. He patented a series of processes which completely changed the methods of manufacturing alum. He established the Pendleton Alum Works, but after a remarkable trial at the Liverpool Assizes in 1857 he removed from there to Newton Heath. As an employer of labour Mr. Spence was exceedingly popular. He was often invited to contest for seats in Parliament, but uniformly declined, preferring to render public service in other ways. He died on July 5th, 1883, at Old Trafford. His efforts as a temperance and social reformer were ably continued by his son, Frank Spence.

And now in closing our references to Oldham Road we will make a few statements as to its residents. It does not appear that at any time the road from New Cross to Newton Heath and Oldham has been favoured as a high class residential district. A century ago bounded by fields, the change from farm land to the site of mills, workshops and their attendant cottages and small shops was direct, and not as in some other districts, gradual. In the case of Harpurhey and Rochdale Road, the change was gradual, as for a time mansions and their gardens occupied the land now given to other classes of property. Oldham Road, so far as the Manchester end was concerned, was never favoured by our merchants as a place for residence. The result has been that, comparatively speaking, there has been a dearth of notable men connected by residence with the road. Forty years ago it was pretty much as it is to-day, and twenty years before that we fail to find a single name of note amongst the long list of those who lived in its houses.

The residents of those days must have been a thirsty lot, for between New Cross and Miles Platting, that is a point just beyond Ash Street, there were seventeen fully licensed houses and twenty-seven beer retailers. One does not wonder when one reads that there were also nearly a dozen pawnshops ; but we should hardly expect to find seven chemist's shops. Mr. E. Rathbone kept a school at number 195, Mr. Handforth had his academy at 261, and at 458 was Heywood's Free School. Concerning the last named institution I have failed to obtain any information, and should be obliged if any reader who knows anything about either the school or its proprietors would communicate with me.

When we consider the district as it is to-day we should hardly have expected to find a farmer amongst its residents of sixty years ago. Jane Royle, farmer, lived at 468, but we have no information as to the extent or situation of the land farmed by her. It would be back land, and the Cow Lane of which we have record would probably be the route taken by the cows on their way to and from the farm and the pasture fields. A few doors away from the farm was the residences of a gardener, another occupation for which there is little demand thereabouts to-day. Of the remainder of the residents of those days little can be said. They passed through life without leaving a record behind them. It may be noted, however, that at number 368 John Whitehead kept a circulating library, and also as denoting another matter in which that generation differ considerably from the present one that in the whole length of the thoroughfare under review there was only one tobacconist's shop. There was at the same time no newspaper shop, no bookseller, and no stationer, in Oldham Road.

Miles Platting is vaguely described as being at the "top of Oldham Road," and the residents according to the directory were few in number or at any rate they included very few whose names were of sufficient importance to be printed. They included Molineux Rothwell & Co, silk manufacturers and Samuel Brewis, jean and satteen manufacturer. One of the partners of the former firm, Richard Rothwell, lived at Miles Platting, near to the mill. Of the four remaining names on the list of residents that of Betty Aspell who was the landlady of the White Hart Tavern was one.

The population of Miles Platting must have been very small in those days, to-day it is about as big as the limitations of space will allow. Never again will the district be even semi-rural in appearance; but it is well to remember that within the memory of persons still living it merited that description.

INDEX.

Lightning Source UK Ltd.
Milton Keynes UK
UKOW01f0839140617
303328UK00001B/68/P